Since 1996, Bloomberg Press has published books for financial professionals, as well as books of general interest in investing, economics, current affairs, and policy affecting investors and business people. Titles are written by well-known practitioners, BLOOMBERG NEWS® reporters and columnists, and other leading authorities and journalists. Bloomberg Press books have been translated into more than 20 languages.

For a list of available titles, please visit our website at www.wiley.com/go/bloombergpress.

BIG MISTAKES

The Best Investors and Their Worst Investments

Michael Batnick

WILEY

Published by John Wiley & Sons, Inc., Hoboken, New Jersey.
Published simultaneously in Canada.

For general information on our other products and services or for technical support, please contact our Customer Care Department within the United States at (800) 762–2974, outside the United States at (317) 572–3993, or fax (317) 572–4002.

Wiley publishes in a variety of print and electronic formats and by print-on-demand. Some material included with standard print versions of this book may not be included in e-books or in print-on-demand. If this book refers to media such as a CD or DVD that is not included in the version you purchased, you may download this material at http://booksupport.wiley.com. For more information about Wiley products, visit www.wiley.com.

Library of Congress Cataloging-in-Publication Data:

Names: Batnick, Michael, 1985- author.
Title: Big mistakes : the best investors and their worst investments /
  Michael Batnick.
Description: Hoboken : Bloomberg Press, 2018. | Series: Bloomberg | Includes
  index. |
Identifiers: LCCN 2018008845 (print) | LCCN 2018011282 (ebook) | ISBN
  9781119366416 (epub) | ISBN 9781119366430 (pdf) | ISBN 9781119366553
  (hardback)
Subjects: LCSH: Investments. | Securities. | BISAC: BUSINESS & ECONOMICS /
  Investments & Securities.
Classification: LCC HG4521 (ebook) | LCC HG4521 .B38 2018 (print) | DDC
  332.6—dc23
LC record available at https://lccn.loc.gov/2018008845

Cover Design: Wiley
Cover Image: © LUHUANFENG / iStockphoto

Printed in the United States of America.

V10001770_062218

To my mother and father who let me make mistakes,
and to Robyn who stuck with me when I made them

CONTENTS

Preface

By three methods may we learn wisdom: First, by reflection, which is noblest; second, by imitation, which is easiest; and third by experience, which is the bitterest.

—Confucius

Making money in the stock market is difficult. Whether you're running a hedge fund or your own brokerage account, there will be times when you feel really foolish. In the event of a market downturn, this misery will be accompanied by others, but other times, you'll be all alone on an island. You might buy a particular stock after it doubled only to see it head south after your purchase, or worse, you will throw in the towel on a loser only to see it double in the next twelve months. Sometimes it can feel as if the market gods are taunting you.

The best way to learn how hard investing can be is to do it for yourself. The second best way, which is the purpose behind this book, is to examine the biggest mistakes committed by the world's most successful investors. From Jesse Livermore to Warren Buffett to Jack Bogle, every investor that has experienced success has experienced equal part failure. There are errors of omission, Buffett and Munger not buying Walmart, and errors of commission, Stanley Druckenmiller buying tech stocks as they reached their peak in early 2000. This book aims to help the reader relate to some of their blunders and understand that temporary setbacks have knocked on all of our doors.

All investors, from Peter Lynch to the average Joe, are hard-wired with human emotions. We're risk averse, we anchor to our purchase point, and we're all manipulated by hindsight bias. And when we experience failure, usually it's self-inflicted, which makes dealing with it objectively a very daunting task. Difficult as it is, we must figure out how to prevent previous mistakes from interfering with future decisions.

People typically strive to replicate success. Kobe Bryant studied Michael Jordan and Paul Tudor Jones studied Jesse Livermore. This makes intuitive sense. Others take a different approach and study stories of failure and try to avoid whatever it is that tripped that person or company up. Like Charlie Munger said, "Tell me where I'm going to die so I never go there." This book takes a different angle altogether, it *focuses* on the most successful investors' failures. The reason is not so that we can say, "Oh, this didn't work, don't do that," but rather so that when we *do* make a mistake, we recognize it for what it is, a part of the game. Perhaps like no other endeavor, learning to invest can only be done through practice. You can no more learn to invest through reading a book than you can read about heart surgery and perform a triple bypass. You just have to do it over and over and over again.

This is not a how-to book. If there is one takeaway, it's that investing is extremely difficult. You will make mistakes. You will repeat them. You will discover new ones. And just when you think you've got it all figured out, the market will humble you once more. It is imperative that you take this in stride, that you don't let these molehills turn into mountains. Once your brain gets poisoned with negative thoughts, it's very difficult to disinfect.

The most important thing successful investors have in common is worrying about what they can control. They don't waste time worrying about which way the market will go or what the Federal Reserve will do or what inflation or interest rates will be next year. They stay within their circle of competence, however narrow that might be. Warren Buffett said, "What counts for most people in investing is not how much they know, but rather how realistically they define what they don't know."

I hope you enjoy reading this as much as I enjoyed writing it.

Michael Batnick

BIG MISTAKES

CHAPTER 1

Benjamin Graham

There Are No Iron-Clad Laws

> In my nearly fifty years of experience in Wall Street I've found that
> I know less and less about what the stock market is going to do
> but I know more and more about what investors ought to do; and
> that's a pretty vital change in attitude.
>
> —Benjamin Graham

In 200 years, nobody will remember Bill Ackman's crusade against Herbalife. John Paulson's bet against the housing bubble will be long forgotten. Charlie's Mungerisms will be relegated to the dustbin of the twenty-first century. Great investors come and go, and most of the ones featured in this book will be lost on future generations. But if I had to put my money on one name that will stand the test of time, it's Benjamin Graham.

The Dean of Wall Street, as he was known, will be remembered forever because his teachings are timeless. The lessons he provided in his seminal work, *Security Analysis*, are just as relevant today as they were in 1934 and will be 200 years hence. The passage of time won't change human nature or the fact that "in applying analysis to the field of securities we encounter the serious obstacle that investment is by nature not an exact science."[1] As gifted as Graham was in mathematics, he understood that the laws of physics do not govern security analysis. It's difficult to overstate how many trails he blazed. Jason Zweig wrote, "Before Graham, money managers behaved much like a medieval guild, guided largely by superstition, guess-work, and arcane rituals."[2] Ben Graham is to investing what the Wright Brothers are to flight, and just as their names will be forever linked to the airplane, so will Graham's to finance.

Graham understood what few did at the time – that the stock prices quoted in the newspaper and the underlying value in the business are not equivalent. Sticking with the Wright brothers, Graham wrote:

> In the Wright Aeronautical example, the earlier situation presented
> a set of facts which demonstrated that the business was worth sub-
> stantially more than $8 per share.... In the later year, the facts were
> equally conclusive that the business did not have a reasonable value
> of $280 per share.... It would have been difficult for the analyst
> to determine whether Wright Aeronautical was actually worth $20
> or $40 a share ... or actually worth $50 or $80.... But fortunately it
> was not necessary to decide these points in order to conclude that the
> shares were attractive at $8 and unattractive, intrinsically, at $280.[3]

Security Analysis was written for the Wall Street professional. However it's *The Intelligent Investor* that will keep Graham's name alive forever. This is the first financial book that I ever read, and it left such a strong impression that I chose it as the namesake for my blog, *The Irrelevant Investor*. Unlike *Security Analysis, The Intelligent Investor* was intended for laymen, and, with more than a million copies sold, it reached its target. Warren Buffett said, "I read the first edition of this book early in 1950, when I was nineteen. I thought then that it was by far the best book about investing ever written. I still think it is."[4] As long as people want to learn about investing, they will find Graham, who translated an exotic language with terms like *net working capital* and *return on equity* into plain English with words like *price* and *value*.

Ben Graham invented the field of financial analysis. Roger Lowenstein said, "Investing without Graham would be like communism without Marx – the disciple would scarcely exist."[5] He was a polymath whom Charlie Munger called "a brilliant man" and "the only intellectual in the investing business at the time."[6] At just 20 years old, in his final semester at Columbia, he was offered three invitations, from the English, mathematics, and philosophy departments. Overwhelmed by these offers, he turned to Columbia's dean for advice. By a stroke of luck, a member of the New York Stock Exchange happened to come in to see the dean at the same time and asked him to recommend one of his strongest students. Without hesitation, he introduced him to Ben Graham.

Graham began his career on Wall Street in 1914, just before the New York Stock Exchange would close for four months, its longest shutdown ever, in light of the events surrounding the Great War. At 20 years old, without having taken any economics courses in college, he started at the bottom of the ladder, delivering securities and checks. After a month, he was promoted as an assistant to the bond department, and just six weeks later, with his advanced intellect, Graham was writing a daily market letter.

Ben Graham taught at Columbia Business School for 28 years, beginning in 1928, and simultaneously taught at the New York Stock Exchange's school, now known as the New York Institute of Finance, for a decade. He attracted students like Walter Schloss, Irving Kahn, and Bill Ruane. His most famous pupil, of course, is Warren Buffett, who became the richest man on the planet by using the principles that Ben Graham taught him.

Graham is on the Mount Rushmore of investing, and despite the enormous success he had managing money and teaching future generations how to do the same, his career, like everybody else's, included some trying times. The lessons that Graham provided in the classroom, which he translated into books, will live forever. But we can also learn a lot from his failures. The most important lesson that investors should take from the person who taught us the difference between value and price is that value investing is not a panacea. Cheap can get cheaper. Rich can get richer. Margins of safety can be miscalculated, and value can fail to materialize.

Some investors search for companies that they expect will grow their earnings significantly faster than the broader market. Others prefer to look for companies whose future prospects aren't nearly as bad as their share prices reflect. Whether you consider yourself a growth investor, a value investor, something in between or entirely different, investors want stocks to be worth more than they pay for it. Value investing is the most effective way to determine whether the price you pay for a slice of the business is less than what the company is actually worth.

When *Security Analysis* was published, the Dow Jones Industrial Average was trading at 100. Today, 84 years later and hovering near 22,000, it's delivered 6.7% a year, not including dividends. Some of the best-known investors, devotees of value investing brought mainstream by Graham, have earned far greater returns by following a few simple rules. These rules all boil down to what Graham referred to as a "margin of safety." Graham defined this as "the discount at which the stock is selling below its minimum intrinsic value."[7] Yes, there were formulas involved, but they didn't need to be complicated. Graham liked stocks selling for one-third less than their net working capital. He once pointed out, "Some extraordinary results could have been obtained since 1933 by buying each year the shares of the six companies in the Dow Jones Industrial Average which sold at the lowest multiplier of their recent earnings."[8]

What made Graham so brilliant is not the calculations he performed to determine intrinsic value, but rather the understanding that determining exact values are both impossible and not a prerequisite for success. "It is quite possible to decide by inspection that a woman is old enough to vote without knowing her age or that a man is heavier than he should be without knowing his exact weight."[9]

Graham was far ahead of his time, writing about behavioral economics, the study of how psychology affects financial decision making, long before the term even existed. *Security Analysis* was published the same year that Nobel laureate Daniel Kahneman, who took this field mainstream, was born. Graham identified some of the cognitive and emotional biases that caused investors to send a strong company diving 50% in 12 months. He examined the case of General Electric, which the stock market valued at $1.87 billion in 1937 and $784 million just one year later. Graham summarized it this way:

> Certainly nothing had happened within twelve months' time to destroy more than half the value of this powerful enterprise, nor did investors even pretend to claim that the falling off in earnings from 1937 to 1938 had any permanent significance for the future of the company. General Electric sold at 64 7/8 because the public was in an optimistic frame of mind and at 27 1/4 because the same people were pessimistic. To speak of these prices as representing "investment values" or the "appraisal of investors" is to do violence either to the English language or to common sense, or both.[10]

Graham taught his students and his readers that prices fluctuate more than value, because it is humans who set price, while businesses set value.

In *The Intelligent Investor*, he summed up the wild swings in price with a story he told about a hypothetical Mr. Market:

> Imagine that in some private business you own a small share that cost you $1,000. One of your partners, named Mr. Market, is very obliging indeed. Every day he tells you what he thinks your interest is worth and furthermore offers either to buy you out or to sell you an additional interest on that basis. Sometimes his idea of value appears plausible and justified by business developments and prospects as you know them. Often, on the other hand, Mr. Market lets his enthusiasm or his fears run away with him, and the value he proposes seems to you little short of silly.[11]

The financial world looks markedly different today than it did when Graham was practicing and teaching. In 1934, a total of 323 million shares were traded on the New York Stock Exchange.[12] As I write, on August 9, 2017, the total volume of shares traded on the NYSE was 3.2 billion. More than 10 times as many shares traded yesterday as all the shares traded during 1934! Today, supercomputers instantly parse the words contained in economic reports and company statements. Back in Graham's times, while quarterly statements were considered standard, they were not the law. And of the companies that made this information available, there was no uniformity; the reports varied from only net earnings to a line itemed income statement and balance sheet. Graham looked for the income statement to contain a minimum of: sales, net earnings, depreciation, interest charges, nonoperating income, income taxes, dividends paid, and surplus adjustments. Prior to the Securities and Exchange Act, less than half of industrial corporations supplied this breakdown.

Graham's idea of value investing involves buying cigar butts, businesses with one final puff, as he called them. These companies controlled significant property, plant and equipment, inventory, and raw materials. It wasn't difficult to measure the tangible assets and calculate the intrinsic value. From there, he could determine whether there was a margin of safety. If Graham were still alive, he wouldn't understand how some companies are valued today. For example, over the last five years, Walmart has earned $75 billion on $2.4 trillion in revenue. Its net margins have been 3.15% and it's *lost* $3.6 billion in market capitalization. Amazon, on the other hand, has earned $3.5 billion on $490 billion of revenue. Its net margins have been 0.73%, and over this time it has added $350 billion in market capitalization.[13] While value investing intuitively makes a lot of sense, human emotions can overwhelm common sense. Prices can be driven both way below liquidating value and far past what any company can reasonably be expected to grow into. While Graham wouldn't recognize ETFs or high-frequency trading, he would feel right at home in today's market, which is still driven by investors' emotions. The way investors behave today, driven by fear and the fear of missing out would be very recognizable to him.

Roger Lowenstein said, "It took Graham 20 years – which is to say, a complete cycle from the bull market of the Roaring Twenties through the dark, nearly ruinous days of the early 1930s – to refine his investment philosophy into a discipline that was as rigorous as the Euclidean theorems he had studied in college."[14] Let's return to the beginning.

Graham first started an investment partnership in 1923, the Graham Corporation, where he would apply arbitrage techniques, the simultaneous purchase of undervalued securities, and short sale of overvalued securities. This operation lasted for two years, and in 1926, he set up the Benjamin Graham Joint Account. In this structure, he would receive 20% of the first 20% return, 30% of the next 30%, and 50% of the balance. In 1926, he earned 32% while the Dow Jones Industrial Average gained just 0.34%. Word of his success spread throughout Wall Street and the famous financier Bernard Baruch asked Graham to become his partner.

Graham was flattered, but having made $600,000 the previous year, he had no reason to accept the invitation.[15] He began with $450,000, which ballooned to $2,500,000 in just three years. But this is a book about lessons we can learn from the failures of the best investors ever. Graham's was right around the corner.

In the final year of the great bull market of the 1920s, the Joint Account gained 60%, outpacing the 49.47% advance in the Dow. In the final months of 1929 when the market turned violently lower, Graham covered his shorts and held onto his convertible preferred securities, thinking that prices were too low and that Mr. Market was talking crazy. He finished the year down 20%, while the Dow fell 17%. Graham was about to learn that margins of safety don't matter when the baby is getting thrown out with the proverbial bathwater.

In 1930, thinking the worst was over, Graham went all in and then some. He used margin to leverage what he thought would be terrific returns. But the worst was not over, and when the Dow collapsed, Graham had his worst year ever, losing 50%. "He personally was wiped out in the crash. Having ducked the 1929 cataclysm, he was enticed back into the market before the final bottom."[16] In the four years from 1929 to the bottom in 1932, Graham lost 70%. If such a careful and thoughtful analyst can lose 70% of his money, we should be very careful to understand that while value investing is a wonderful option over the long term, it is not immune to the short-term vicissitudes of the market.

In 1932, just weeks before stocks bottomed, Graham wrote three articles in *Forbes*. In one, "Inflated Treasuries and Deflated Stockholders," he wrote:

> There are literally dozens of other companies which also have a quoted value less than their cash in bank. . . . This means that a great number of American businesses are quoted in liquidating value; that in the best recent judgment of Wall Street, these businesses are worth more dead than alive.[17]

In this article, Ben Graham was a voice of reason in a mob of financially depressed zombies:

> It is time, and high time, that the millions of American shareholders turned their eyes from the daily market reports long enough to give some attention to the enterprises themselves of which they are the proprietors, and which exist for their benefit and at their pleasure.[18]

After an 89% peak-to-trough decline in the Dow Jones Industrial Average, it was understandable why people would behave this way, and why a generation of investors would never return to the market. The fact that he remained steadfast in his conviction that security analysis was a worthwhile endeavor is nothing short of remarkable.

The partnership earned 6% a year from 1926 to 1935, compared to 5.8% for the S&P 500 and 3.8% for the Dow.[19] Despite the hard times and enormous drawdown, Graham would continue to operate under the assumption that value investing is the most intelligent way to achieve superior results. Believing that stocks eventually find their true value, the prospectus of Graham-Newman Corporation's stated that its investment policy is "To purchase securities at less than their intrinsic value as determined by careful analysis, with particular emphasis on purchase of securities at less than their liquidating value."[20] When asked what causes a stock to find its value, Graham answered, "That is one of the mysteries of our business, and it is a mystery to me as well as to everybody else. We know from experience that eventually the market catches up with value. It realizes it in one way or another."[21] Graham was proven right; over the long, long term, buying cheap stocks is a great strategy. Graham-Newman would outperform the market by nearly 3% a year for 20 years, a record that very few people have ever achieved.[22]

The fact that investors are willing to pay as little as five times for the prior 12 months' worth of earnings, and as much as 34, shows that relying on valuation alone is not enough. If you're not a dyed-in-the-wool value investor, and even if you are, surviving the long periods of time when the market separates price from value, on the upside and on the downside, can be mentally exhausting. You have the right to pay whatever you feel is fair value for stocks. Think 25 times trailing 12-month earnings is too high a price? Want to go all in at 10 times? Okay, but understand that waiting for valuations to "normalize" has stained the legacy of some of the greatest value investors to ever live. You can read all about the mood swings of Mr. Market, but that doesn't make you Dr. Freud.

Even though Graham pioneered security analysis, he was humble and open minded to the idea that what used to work no longer works, and what works today might not work as well in the future. He said:

> Unfortunately in this kind of work, where you are trying to determine relationships based upon past behavior, the almost invariable experience is that by the time you have had a long enough period to give

you sufficient confidence in your form of measurement just then new conditions supersede and the measurement is no longer dependable in the future.[23]

Value investing still "works," but because it used to work so incredibly well, it has seen an influx of aspiring Warren Buffetts. This has made it much more challenging to identify undervalued opportunities. Graham recognized this dynamics long before this was a widely held belief. In a 1976 interview he said:

> I am no longer an advocate of elaborate techniques of security analysis in order to find superior value opportunities. This was a reward-ing activity, say, forty years ago, when our textbook "Graham and Dodd" was first published; but the situation has changed a good deal since then. In the old days any well-trained security analyst could do a good professional job of selecting undervalued issues through detailed studies; but in the light of the enormous amount of research now being carried on, I doubt whether in most cases such exten-sive efforts will generate sufficiently superior selections to justify their costs. To that very limited extent I'm on the side of the "efficient market" school of thought now generally accepted by professors.[24]

He was asked whether "Wall Street professionals are usually more accu-rate in their near or long-term market trends, forecasts of stock market trends, if not, why not?" With a smile on his face, he answered:

> Well, we've been following that interesting question for a generation or more and I must say frankly our studies indicate you have your choice of tossing coins and taking the consensus of expert opinion, and the results are just about the same in each case. Your question is to why they are not more dependable is a very good one and an inter-esting one and my own explanation for that is this; that everybody in Wall Street is so smart that their brilliance offsets each other. And that whatever they know is already reflected in the level of stock prices pretty much and consequently what happens in the future represents what they don't know.[25]

It's critically important to be aware of value, but it's more important not to be a slave to it. Graham taught us that there are no iron-clad laws in finance and that cheap can get cheaper.

Like every lesson we'll come across in this book, the unfortunate reality is most of these have to be learned the hard way. Nobody can tell you that picking stocks is hard and that you're better off in an index fund. You'll never believe that a stock that falls 50% in a year might not necessarily be a bargain. You have to catch a few of these falling knives before scars develop and you learn that a falling price might not equate to better value. Many of the investors covered in this book began with Ben Graham's teachings, but they, like you, had to discover their own paths.

Notes

1. Benjamin Graham and David L. Dodd, *Security Analysis* (New York: McGraw-Hill Education, 2008), 61.
2. Jason Zweig, "A Note about Benjamin Graham," in *The Intelligent Investor* by Benjamin Graham (New York: HarperBusiness, 2003), xi.
3. Graham and Dodd, *Security Analysis*, 67.
4. Warren Buffett, "Preface to the Fourth Edition," in *The Intelligent Investor* by Benjamin Graham (New York: HarperBusiness, 2003), ix.
5. Quoted in Roger Lowenstein, *Buffett: The Making of an American Capitalist* (New York: Random House, 2008), 36.
6. Quoted in Rupert Hargreaves, "Why Charlie Munger Hates Value Investing," Nasdaq.com, April 13, 2017.
7. Graham and Dodd, *Security Analysis*, 373.
8. Benjamin Graham, "Securities in an Insecure World" (speech given at Town Hall at St. Francis Hotel, San Francisco, CA, November 15, 1963).
9. Graham and Dodd, *Security Analysis*, 66.
10. Ibid., 30.
11. Benjamin Graham, *The Intelligent Investor* (New York: HarperBusiness, 2003).
12. New York Stock Exchange, "Daily Share Volume 1930–1939."
13. Data provided by Ycharts, author's calculations.
14. Roger Lowenstein, "Introduction to Part I," in *Security Analysis*, 6th ed., by Benjamin Graham and David L. Dodd (New York: McGraw-Hill Education, 2008), 41.
15. Irving Kahn and Robert D. Milne, "Benjamin Graham: The Father of Financial Analysis" (Charlottesville, VA: Financial Analysts Research Foundation, 1977).
16. John Train, *Money Masters of Our Time* (New York: HarperBusiness, 2003).

17. Benjamin Graham, "Inflated Treasuries and Deflated Stockholders," *Forbes*, June 1, 1932.

18. Ibid.

19. Kahn and Milne, "Benjamin Graham," 42.

20. Benjamin Graham and Jerome A. Newton, Letter to Graham-Newton Corporation stockholders, January 31, 1946.

21. Ibid.

22. Roger Lowenstein, *Buffett: The Making of an American Capitalist* (New York: Random House, 2008), p. 58.

23. Jason Zweig, "A Rediscovered Masterpiece by Benjamin Graham," JasonZweig.com, March 31, 2015.

24. Benjamin Graham, "A Conversation with Benjamin Graham," *Financial Analysts Journal* 32, no. 5 (September/October 1976): 20–23.

25. "Legacy of Benjamin Graham: The Original Adjunct Professor," Heilbrunn Center for Graham and Dodd Investing, Columbia Business School, February 1, 2013.

CHAPTER 2

Jesse Livermore

Manage Your Risk

Jesse Livermore was a larger-than-life, full-blooded character who happened to embody every great trading maxim of the time.
—Paul Tudor Jones

"Buy low, sell high."

"Nobody ever went broke taking a profit."

"Buy when there's blood in the streets."

We often use these axioms to justify why we bought, sold, or held onto an investment. The problem with rules of thumb, specifically when it comes to investing, is that they mask complexity. There are far too many variables and crosscurrents pushing and pulling on the price of a security to boil everything down to a cute little phrase. Doing this can lead to systematic biases, blind spots and bad decisions that are repeated again and again. Consider the following example from Daniel Kahneman's *Thinking, Fast and Slow*:

> Steve is very shy and withdrawn, invariably helpful but with little interest in people or in the world of reality. A meek and tidy soul, he has a need for order and structure, and a passion for detail. Is Steve more likely to be a librarian or a farmer?
>
> The resemblance of Steve's personality to that of a stereotypical librarian strikes everyone immediately, but equally relevant statistical considerations are almost always ignored.... Because there are so many more farmers, it is almost certain that more "meek and tidy" souls will be found on tractors than at library information desks. However, we found that participants in our experiments ignored the relevant statistical facts and relied exclusively on resemblance. We proposed that they used resemblance as a simplifying heuristic (roughly, a rule of thumb) to make a difficult judgment. The reliance on the heuristic caused predictable biases (systematic errors) in their predictions.[1]

Think about how this sort of thinking manifests itself in investing. There are so many variables that you almost *have* to use shortcuts and sayings. And nobody's words or sayings are repeated more often than Jesse Livermore. For example: "Speculation is as old as the hills. Whatever happened in the stock market today has happened before and will happen again." And: "They said there are two sides to everything. But there is only one side to the stock market; and it's not the bull side or the bear side, but the right side."

If you're a trader, concerned primarily with being on the right side, keeping things simple can be overwhelming. Where are stocks going and which direction are they coming from? Are they being led higher (lower) by a narrowing group of stocks, or is there broad participation? How bullish (bearish) are investors? Is my own portfolio keeping me from answering this objectively? The list goes on and on. And while it's true that simplifying things generally leads to better decisions, it's *not* true that every situation can be condensed into a saying. No investor is more emblematic of the dangers of heuristics than Jesse Livermore, who made and lost several fortunes, and each time came away with beautifully elegant analysis.

Jesse Livermore is the most famous, *maybe the first famous*, market speculator. The lesson that investors should learn from Livermore is how dangerous rules of thumb can be. If you catch yourself saying "buy when there is blood in the streets," it's a good idea to remember that the man who basically invented market phrases couldn't even stick to them. Buy low, sell high sounds great, and the idea is, but like many things, it's easy to say, hard to do.

Jesse Livermore, or JL, as his friends knew him, was born and raised on a farm in Acton, Massachusetts, in 1877. At 14, he left home for the big city—Boston—where he quickly got a job at Paine Webber as a board boy, earning $6 a week.

While he was learning about the market, young Livermore kept a journal, recording fictional trades. After 18 months of preparation, he visited a bucket shop, which were places where investors, mostly amateurs, could trade. His first purchase was Chicago, Burlington and Quincy Railroad, and with a $10 investment, he netted $3.12 in just two days.[2] He was immediately successful, and by 17, he built up a bankroll of $1,200. He had tasted the spoils of success and wanted more of it. He decided to leave Paine Webber and pursue speculating full time.

Bucket shops were used to traders leaving with empty pockets, and the traders who made money did not do so for long without the bosses taking notice. He became a victim of his own success, and before long, he was persona non grata in every bucket shop in Boston.

Livermore accumulated a bankroll and a few years of experience when he was forced to leave Boston if he wanted to continue trading. He already suffered his first big loss, which would become a recurring theme throughout his life.

Livermore left Boston for New York in 1900 when he was 23 years old. The same day he arrived, he walked into the offices of the brokerage house, Harris, Hutton & Company, run by 25-year-old Edward Hutton, who would later go on to found E.F. Hutton.[3] Hutton and Livermore immediately hit it off. JL deposited his $2,500 and was extended another $22,500 of credit, allowing him to drop $25,000 into the market.

Stocks were acting very favorable and on the right side of the tape, Livermore made $50,000 in less than a week. But the difference between amateur and professional trading, which he would soon learn, is like the difference between driving a racecar simulator and getting behind the wheel of a Porsche 917.

> In a bucket shop, the ticker price was the price which shares were bought and sold. But it was not the actual price on the stock exchange floor. The world of the bucket shop revolved around the ticker price rather than the reality of the floor price. On the real stock exchange, the ticker was only the communication medium, and the real price being quoted on the floor exchange could be very different.[4]

In May 1901, JL would experience his first large loss as a professional speculator, this time from the short side. Shorting is the opposite of buying, and this suited Livermore, a natural skeptic, perfectly. Rather than buy low, sell high, the short seller is attempting to sell high, buy back low and pocket the difference.

On a Monday before the market opened, Livermore put in orders to short 1,000 shares of U.S. Steel at $100 and 1,000 shares of Santa Fe Railroad at $80. He had used up his entire capital and was levered 4:1. In other words, the margin for error was paper-thin. His orders weren't filled at $100 and $80, but instead at $85 and $65, which is where he intended to cover! (Close his short position.) And when the market went against him, he couldn't get out fast enough and the leverage buried him. JL lost $50,000 in just a few hours. At 23, he was broke. In fact, he was worse than broke, he actually owed his employers $500.

He realized what was going on, that the lessons and experience he took from the bucket shops didn't necessarily translate to professional trading. *"The tape always spoke ancient history to me, as far as my system of trading went, and I didn't realize it."*[5]

Livermore was an excellent client for the firm and Harris, Hutton offered to credit his account $1,000, but JL didn't accept their offer. He knew he wasn't ready yet to play in the big leagues so he decided to return to the amateurs, where he knew he could win.

The problem was that all of the bucket shops in New York had closed, and he wasn't welcome at any in Boston. So he went to St. Louis where nobody could spot him. Livermore slid right back into his old ways and made $2,800 in just two days. But on his third day, as he tried to make an order, he was told the boss wanted to see him. "Horace Kent," the name he gave, was figured out to be the infamous "Boy Plunger," Jesse Livermore.[6]

Out of options, he returned to New York, repaid his $500 debt, and was left with $2,000 to trade.

"The training of a stock trader is like a medical education. The physician had to spend long years learning."[7] Over the next few years, Livermore paid his dues, putting in the time, getting an education and building a bankroll. At 28, he had accumulated $100,000 but hadn't yet had his first big score.

While he was vacationing in Palm Beach, for no reason other than a hunch, he decided to sell 1,000 shares short of Union Pacific. Not satisfied, he went back and sold another 1,000 shares, and then another 1,000 shares, and by the end of the day, was short 3,000 shares and down $7,500.

The next morning he woke up and sold another 2,000 shares. Having built up a large position, he decided it was time to head back to New York where he could better monitor his positions.

Twenty-five hundred miles away, an earthquake hit San Francisco, lasting 42 seconds and shaking the ground over a distance of 296 miles. Three hundred seventy-five people were killed, and 277,000 others were left homeless within the first week. Livermore was convinced that this would break the market in his favor, but the market didn't seem to mind. So, Livermore doubled his position, shorting another 5,000 shares at first, and then he decided to go for broke, doubling his position again. He called this patience "sitting" and attributed it to his success, despite being a difficult strategy to master. His sitting paid off big time when on Friday, April 20, the market finally cracked. On Saturday, he covered his entire stake, making $250,000, over $6 million in today's dollars. Jesse Livermore was a rich man.

He decided to sit back for a while and enjoy his first big score. But he couldn't help himself and was back in the market before no time, again jumping in on the short side. After several big losses, he quickly watched 90% of his recent windfall evaporate. As usual, he was very clearheaded in his analysis. *"I had made a mistake. But where? I was bearish in a bear market. That was wise, and I had sold stocks short. That was proper. But I had sold them too soon, and that was costly. My position was right, but my play was wrong."*[8]

Livermore quickly rebounded, as he was known to do, and over the next few months, shorting into rallies, he made back everything he lost and then some, accumulating a bankroll of $750,000.

In 1907, Augustus and Otto Heinze, along with Charles Morse, tried to corner United Copper (gain control of the stock). Their attempt failed, which sent the shares crashing down from $60 to $10 within a few days. It forced all three financiers into bankruptcy. They borrowed a lot of money from trust companies in their attempt to corner the market, and when they went bust, a run on the banks followed, which triggered a panic.

When the collapse arrived, Livermore was short and on paper had gains of $1,000,000. But there was no liquidity and certainly nobody to buy his shares, and he wasn't confident that he would ever collect his profits. But when JP Morgan came in and provided the market with liquidity and confidence, he covered his shorts and made a fortune.

By the end of 1907, and before his 30th birthday, Livermore was worth $3 million. But once again, not content to rest on his laurels, he decided to take his commodity trading to the next level. In 1908, he moved to Chicago to trade commodities full time. His first play was in cotton, where he accumulated a huge position, 140,000 bales, and earned almost $2 million. This earned him legendary status and a new nickname, the Cotton King.

By the middle of 1908, fresh off a huge score, he returned to New York, with $5 million in his bank account.

His success in cotton attracted Teddy Price, one of the most famous and well-regarded cotton speculators in the world. Price told JL he wanted to partner with him; the idea was he would supply the pertinent fundamental information and JL would trade it. Livermore quickly shot down this idea.

While Livermore was not interested in a partnership, he didn't mind developing a friendship, and the two became very close. They were vacationing together in Palm Beach, and JL was captivated and seduced by all that Price knew about the world of commodities. But Livermore was a tape reader, and fundamental factors like the size and the quality of the crop were of little importance to him. But Price's knowledge was so sharp and so seductive that it infected Livermore's brain. JL was bearish on cotton, and Price was on the other side. Convinced he couldn't have known more than Price, JL covered his shorts and even started buying. He quickly accumulated 160,000 bales of cotton.

While he was buying cotton, he was also long wheat, which showed a nice profit. Disregarding his own rules, the ones that he spent years developing, he sold his winner and added to his loser. *"Always sell what shows you a loss and keep what shows you a profit. That was so obviously the wise thing to do and was so well known to me that even now I marvel at myself for doing the reverse."*

This one hurt. He had made a mistake that was so obvious in real time and especially in hindsight. *"It seems incredible that knowing the game as well as I did, and with an experience of twelve or fourteen years of speculating in stocks and commodities, I did precisely the wrong thing."*

To add insult to injury, his "partner" Price double-crossed him. He went short cotton while Livermore kept buying. At the end, JL was carrying 440,000 bales, worth in excess of $25 million. He got crushed, losing $4.5 million.

Livermore once said, *"A man must believe in himself and his judgment if he expects to make a living at this game. That is why I don't believe in tips. If I buy stocks on Smith's tip. I must sell those stocks on Smith's tip.... No sir, nobody can make big money on what someone else tells him to do."* This time he was really disgusted with himself, for it wasn't just being on the wrong side of the trade or having the market turn against him, this time he was directly responsible for his blunder. He violated one of the first rules of trading that he ever learned.

In 1909, he was wiped out completely. He hit a cold streak, and everything he touched turned into a loser:

> I kept trading – and losing. I persisted in thinking that the stock market must make money for me in the end. But the only end in sight was the end of my resources.

Livermore caught a break when he received an offer from a brokerage house to trade with a line of $25,000. The Boy Plunger had a reputation as an aggressive short seller, and the brokerage wanted people to know he was trading there, so that their big clients wouldn't be suspected of dumping large blocks of stock.

He quickly turned that $25,000 into $125,000, but the good times, as was becoming routine, were short-lived. When he tried to sell short 8,000 shares of Baltimore, Chesapeake & Atlantic, the senior broker called him into his office and said, "Jesse, don't do anything in Chesapeake & Atlantic just now. That was a bad play of yours, selling eight thousand short. I covered it for you this morning in London and went long."[9] This went on for months, and the broker kept buying more railroad stock under Jesse's name. He finally realized that he was being used, that one of the senior broker's clients was dying and had a lot of rail stock to sell. And it was bought by Livermore as the prices kept going lower and lower.

For the second time, Livermore had been taken for a ride, and this time, he was simply unable to get out from under the dark cloud. Over the next few years, he accumulated debts of over $1 million, which he wasn't able to repay. At 38 years old, he declared bankruptcy.

Determined to jump back in with a clean slate, Livermore needed a lifeline, a loan of some sort, but he could not incur any fresh debt according to the details of his bankruptcy. He decided to go back to the broker who had fleeced him six years earlier. He was turned down, but was told, when you see something you like, you can buy 500 shares. He watched the market and waited for the perfect opportunity. He bought Bethlehem Steel, and in just two days, he earned $38,000. Markets were acting favorably and he quickly racked up a $200,000 roll.

Stocks exploded higher in World War I, and 1915 was the best year ever for the Dow, gaining 82%. Stocks doubled in less than two years, and he was once again on the right side, bullish in a bull market. A year shy of his 40th birthday, Jesse Livermore was back.

Once the war ended in November 1918, he switched from trading stocks to trading commodities. He set up a whole formal operation and was on top of the world, earning $3 million a year through 1923, and by the end of the year, he had accumulated 20 million bucks. During the roaring, 1920s, he was a cautious bear more than an optimistic bull. He started shorting as early as 1927, just putting out some feelers and taking small losses along the way.

By the fall of 1929, Livermore built up his biggest short position ever, $450 million spread across 100 stocks. And he was about to receive the biggest payday of his entire life. From October 25 through November 13, the Dow crashed 32%. In those 11 days, the Dow fell 5% seven times. Livermore covered all of his shorts and was worth $100 million, equivalent to $1.4 billion in today's dollars. He was one of the richest people in the world.

This would be the height of his powers.

The stock market finally bottomed in July 1932. The crash left nothing unscathed, the stock market was worth just 11% of what it was three years ago. When the bottom arrived, the rubber band had been stretched so far that stocks experienced the greatest snapback bounce ever, even to this day. Over the next 42 days, the Dow gained 93%, but this time, Livermore was on the wrong side. He got crushed. And after covering his shorts, he made his final mistake, going long at the top. That bounce would prove to be of the "dead cat" variety, and stocks came crashing back down, losing nearly 40% from September 1932 through February 1933. Everything he had made in the crash was gone.

Being on the bear side when he should have been on the bull side and then flipping to the bull side when he should have stayed on the bear side cost him everything. By 1934, he was broke again, and owed $5 million to 30 creditors.

He declared bankruptcy for the second time, and over the next few years, he barely scraped by. He was having a real hard time adjusting to the rules imposed by the newly created Securities and Exchange Commission. Many of his tricks and strategies were now illegal and came with hefty punishment.

Livermore once reflected:

All my life I have made mistakes, but in losing money I have gained experience and accumulated a lot of valuable "Don'ts." I have been flat broke several times, but my loss has never been a total loss. Otherwise, I wouldn't be here now. I always knew I would have another chance and that I would not make the same mistake a second time. I believed in myself.[10]

But in 1939 his final attempt at a comeback fell short, he was unable to pull off another miracle, and he was out of opportunities. On November 29, 1940, he took his own life. Court records show that his assets, listed at $107,047, were several hundred thousand dollars less than his liabilities, which totaled $463,517.

It is somewhat ironic that the most quoted trader of all time exhibited such poor risk management. All the sayings and lessons he learned didn't save him from blowing up four times. The real lesson that Livermore learned, too late in life, was that:

If a man is both wise and lucky, he will not make the same mistake twice. But he will make any one of the ten thousand brothers or cousins of the original. The mistake family is so large that there is always one of them around when you want to see what you can do in the fool-play line.[11]

Investing is inherently an act of uncertainty, so we can never say to ourselves, "I'll never let that happen again!" Sure, there are very specific mistakes that you won't repeat, like buying a triple-levered inverse ETF and holding it for three months. That's something you do one time and never repeat. But like Livermore said, the mistake family is too large to avoid all of them. And no amount of market quotes will change the fact that losing money is a part of investing. Risk management is a part of investing. Repeating mistakes is part of investing. It's all part of investing.

If you focus on avoiding unforced errors, you won't need to rely on cute market phrases that sound really great but only provide a false sense of security.

Notes

1. Daniel Kahneman, *Thinking, Fast and Slow* (New York: Farrar, Straus and Giroux, 2013), 7.
2. Tom Rubython, *Jesse Livermore – Boy Plunger* (Dorset, England: Myrtle Press, 2015), 24.
3. Ibid., 49.
4. Ibid., 51–53.
5. Edwin Lefèvre, *Reminiscences of a Stock Operator* (Hoboken, NJ: Wiley), 2006.
6. Rubython, *Jesse Livermore*, 61.
7. Lefèvre, *Reminiscences of a Stock Operator*.
8. Ibid.
9. Rubython, *Jesse Livermore*, 169.
10. Ibid.
11. Ibid.

CHAPTER 3

Mark Twain

Don't Get Attached

If you get into anybody far enough, you've got yourself a partner.
—Mark Twain

When dollars are transferred from our pocket to an investment, the expectation is that they'll be worth more in the future. But when the results disappoint, we're loath to admit we were wrong. Our natural tendency is to hold onto the losers longer than we should, because in doing so, we are deferring defeat and keeping our ego intact.

The problem with small losses is that it's easy to hold onto them as they morph into big losses. In the world of finance, nothing springs eternal like hope. We'll watch with indifference as a 5% loss becomes a 10% loss, with fear as it cascades to a 20% loss, and with utter terror as it falls any further. At this point, we become paralyzed as adrenaline rushes through the 100 billion nerve cells in our brain. The hypothalamus, our "fight or flight" system, suspends rational thinking.

"I'll get out when I'm even." Anybody who has ever bought a stock has experienced this poisonous thought floating between their ears. The unfortunate reality about declines is that the math required to make them whole requires extraordinary acts. A 20% loss requires not a 20% gain to break even, but rather a 25% advance. The deeper the hole, the harder it is to climb out; an 80% loss requires a 400% gain to make your money back.

The hedge fund manager David Einhorn has a great line to describe the danger of holding onto losers: "What do you call a stock that's down 90%? A stock that was down 80% and then got cut in half."[1] In other words, just because a stock fell from $100 to $20, that doesn't mean it can't easily fall to $10.

When our positions go against us, it's easy to hold on, but it's even easier to compound the problem by adding to the position. If you felt good about buying this stock at $100, chances are you'll find it even more attractive at $90. But the problem is so many stocks *never* come back. In fact, since 1980, 40% of stocks experienced a 70% decline from which they never recovered.[2] Adding to a losing position has been the downfall of many investors.

Most people know Samuel Clemens by his pen name, Mark Twain. And most people know Mark Twain as a humorist and as an author. But it was Samuel Clemens, the name he went by his whole life, who sunk Mark Twain's fortunes. In *Chasing the Last Laugh*, author Richard Zacks writes, "Twain was an abysmal investor, an absolute magnet for con men and fool schemes."[3] Peter Krass, author of *Ignorance, Confidence, and Filthy*

Rich Friends, wrote, "The highest paid writer in America had succeeded in losing his entire fortune and the fortune of his coal heiress wife through appalling investments."[4]

Twain traveled great lengths to get back to even because he never learned the about the law of holes, which says, "If you find yourself in a hole, stop digging." He poured $170,000 – $5 million in today's dollars – into what he hoped would become a revolutionary machine.

Although his investments delivered him constant stress, they provided the world with some brilliant language:

> "There are two times in a man's life when he should not speculate, when he can't afford it, and when he can."
>
> "A banker is a fellow who lends you his umbrella when the sun is shining and wants it back the minute it begins to rain."
>
> "That would have been foresight, whereas hindsight is my specialty."
>
> "I was seldom able to see an opportunity until it had ceased to be one."

Ernest Hemingway once said, "All modern American literature comes from one book by Mark Twain called *Huckleberry Finn*." Twain began this project in 1876, but it would be nearly a decade until he'd finish it. This book, which he thought would take two months to write, took a back seat to more important things, like his search for riches.

Mark Twain compiled a list of failed investments longer than a pharmacy receipt. He tried his hand at gold mining, both with a shovel and with stock certificates. Jaded by the experience he said, "A mine is a hole in the ground with a liar standing next to it."

Twain was particularly smitten with inventors. He put money into the New York Vaporizing Co., which was going to improve steam engines, except of course it didn't. Not only did it fail to accomplish its objective, but he provided an endless stream of funds to the inventor, $35 weekly. Twain recalled, "He visited me every few days to report progress and I early noticed by his breath and gait that he was spending 36 dollars a week on whisky, and I could never figure out where he got the other dollar."[5]

Twain invested in Plasmon, a milk powder extract, a steam pulley and a start-up insurance company called the Hartford Accident Insurance Company. He became so fed up with these money-losing ventures that he wrote to a fellow author, "If your books tell how to exterminate inventors send me nine editions."

He also lost plenty of money the old-fashioned way, by buying stocks and selling at the wrong time. One of many examples was the Oregon Transcontinental Railroad, which he purchased at $78 a share and sold at $12. Of this experience, he said, "I don't wish to ever look at a stock report again."[6]

These experiences led him to not only errors of commission but errors of omission, which perhaps burned an even deeper hole of resentment into his soul. He wasted $42,000 on an engraving process called a kaolotype that was supposed to revolutionize illustrations (it didn't), and then decided to pass on Alexander Graham Bell's telephone. A friend of Twain's, General Joseph Roswell Hawley, owned the *Hartford Courant* newspaper and met with Bell. Hawley invited Twain to come to the *Courant* office to hear Bell's pitch to potential investors. As Twain described it, Bell "believed there was great fortune in store for it and wanted me to take some stock. I declined. I said I didn't want anything more to do with wildcat speculation. Then he offered the stock to me at twenty-five. I said I didn't want it at any price."[7]

When he returned from a European vacation, he saw an old clerk in town who had invested the little money he had with Bell, and became a very wealthy man. Twain came back and said, "It is strange the way the ignorant and inexperienced so often and so undeservedly succeed when the informed and the experienced fail."[8] If this strikes you as sour grapes, that's exactly what this is. Mark Twain may have had experience with investing, but it was only with a multitude of failed investments. And to say he was *informed* would have taken giant liberties with the English language.

Twain didn't just invest in others; he had plenty of his own ideas: an elastic strap for holding up pants, a scrapbook with preglued pages, and a portable calendar. Samuel Charles Webster, his niece's husband, once wrote, "He tried to be an Edison as well as a Shakespeare and a few other great men besides."[9]

Twain gambled when he had very little money, and it didn't end once he acquired a great deal of it. The money he had to speculate on some of the bigger failures came from the success he found at Webster & Company, a publishing house which he started in 1885.

Grant's memoirs was the first deal they made, and it was a massive success, breaking records with 600,000 volumes issued. Grant's family received $400,000, $12 million in today's dollars, because of an overly generous deal.[10] Industry royalty standards were 10% of the cover price, but Twain offered him 70% of net profits, after printing expenses and everything. Despite the lousy business deal with the former president, Webster & Company got off to a very good start. Like most things in his life, this too would end badly and what would grind his company's success, and his life, to a screeching halt, was a loss that Twain refused to take. He kept throwing good money after bad, and it inflicted far more damage than all his other losses combined.

James Paige received a patent on his typesetter in 1874, and he envisioned the 18,000-piece machine replacing a similar human-operated apparatus. He met Mark Twain in 1880 and convinced him – although it's likely not much convincing was needed – to invest in what was another horribly crafted contract. Twain was entitled to profits *only* if he paid for all expenses until the completion of the machine, and later, to make matters worse, he promised to pay Paige $7,000 a year until the machine turned a profit. Twain was blinded by his own hubris; he called Paige "the Shakespeare of mechanical invention."

As time went on and money went out, Twain said of Paige: "He could persuade a fish to come out and take a walk with him. When he is present I always believe him: I can't help it. When he is gone away all the belief evaporates. He is a most daring and majestic liar."[11] Toward the end of the nineteenth century, the country experienced its worst economic depression up until that time. During the panic of 1893, 500 banks failed and 15,000 were sent to the graveyard. Twain and Webster & Company wouldn't be spared.

No matter how many times Twain told himself that he was done with Paige and his excuses, he just couldn't look in the mirror and admit he was wrong. Imagine pouring everything you have, financially, mentally, and emotionally, into an investment and admitting defeat. It is excruciating. Few things are harder to do in life and especially in investing than to admit you were wrong. With the help of a friend, Henry "Hell Hound" Rogers, a mega-rich partner in John Rockefeller's Standard Oil, they took control of the typesetter business from Paige. On life support, Clemens went to look for new investors and found two in Bram Stoker, who would later go on to write *Dracula*, and the famous actor Henry Irving.[12]

When the typesetter failed at the *Chicago Herald*, there would be no more chances. Henry Rogers was a serious businessman and, unlike Twain, had no problem cutting his losses. It wasn't as easy for Twain, however, who was traveling in France when he heard of the machine's unraveling.

He wrote Rogers an overly morose letter that indicated he felt connected to the machine almost as though it were a person.

On December 21, 1894, the Paige Compositor Manufacturing Company was laid to rest. In the end, only an outsider had the ability to cut Twain's losses. Without Rogers, it's entirely possible that Twain would have taken this bottomless money pit to his grave. The total loss for the typesetter is estimated to be close to $5 million in today's dollars. Twain's compulsion to keep the typesetter afloat drained his financial resources and was a major reason why Webster & Company couldn't survive the depression. Twain wrote, "I am terribly tired of business. I am by nature unfitted for it and I want to get out of it."

The panic had reduced his stock and bond portfolio from $100,000 to virtually nothing at all. On April 18, 1894, out of options and out of money, Webster & Company declared bankruptcy.

Helen Keller said, "Sometimes it seemed as if he let loose all the artillery of Heaven against an intruding mouse." So you can imagine how Twain felt when the newspapers started to attack him. His spectacular failings in the market produced a series of brilliantly crafted words – "October. This is one of the peculiarly dangerous months to speculate in stocks. The others are July, January, September, April, November, May, March, June, December, August and February."A newspaper took this line and replaced "to speculate in stocks" with "for an author to go into business."He was getting it from all sides. The *San Francisco Call* wrote "Mark Twain's failure was his own fault and yet he plans to lecture the world about it." Twain was hypersensitive of public opinion. He once said, "The public is the only critic whose judgment is worth anything at all."Bombarded with criticism, Twain responded the only way he knew how, with his pen and a canvas:

> It has been reported that I sacrificed, for the benefit of the creditors, the property of the publishing whose financial backer I was, and that I am now lecturing for my own benefit. This is an error. I intend the lectures, as well as the property, for the creditors. The law recognizes no mortgage on a man's brain, and a merchant who has given up all he has may take advantage of the rules of insolvency and start free again for himself; but I am not a business man; and honor is a harder master than the law. It cannot compromise for less than a hundred cents on the dollar, and its debts never outlaw.[13]

At the ripe age of 59, he set out to repay his debts to each and every one of his 101 creditors who made a claim in his bankruptcy filings. In order to get out of the hole, he traveled around the globe doing a standup comedy tour.

He went across the United States, to Australia, New Zealand, India, South Africa, and Europe. By 1898, he was out of debt, and more than ready for new financial adventures.

Twain erased his debts, but he never lost his speculative gene. He said to his friend Rogers, who made him a great deal of money in the stock market, "Don't leave me out; I want to be in, with the other capitalists."

Risk and reward go together like copy and paste; there cannot be one without the other. But sometimes we receive the rewards and other time we experience only the risk. When risk arrives at our brokerage account, which it inevitably does from time to time, don't bury your head in the sand, acknowledge it. The most important thing when speculating is that you keep your losses manageable. Paper cuts sting, but they heal. Shotgun wounds on the other hand, those are tough to come back from.

The best way to avoid the catastrophic losses is to decide before you invest how much you're willing to lose, either in percentage or dollar terms. This way, your decisions will be driven by logic rather than fear—or some other emotional attachment to a position.

Just a few years removed from his bankruptcy, Twain invested $16,000, with high hopes as always, in the American Mechanical Cashier Company. After eight months with no results, after promise after promise and a feeling of déjà vu, he walked away. Lesson learned.

Notes

1. Quoted in Meena Krishnametty, "David Einhorn Told You to Buy GM," MarketWatch.com, December 20, 2012.
2. J. P. Morgan, "The Agony and the Ecstasy," *Eye on the Market: Special Edition*, September 2014.
3. Richard Zacks, *Chasing the Last Laugh* (New York: Doubleday, 2016).
4. Peter Krass, *Ignorance, Confidence, and Filthy Rich Friends* (Hoboken, NJ: Wiley, 2007).
5. Zacks, *Chasing the Last Laugh*, 3.
6. Ibid., 14.

7. Quoted in Elston Electric Company, "Mark Twain and the Telephone," OldTelephones.com, May 29, 2012.

8. Ibid.

9. Krass, *Ignorance, Confidence, and Filthy Rich Friends*, 91.

10. Zacks, *Chasing the Last Laugh*, 6.

11. Krass, *Ignorance, Confidence, and Filthy Rich Friends*, 197.

12. Ibid., 201.

13. Quoted in Zacks, *Chasing the Last Laugh*, 67–70.

CHAPTER 4

John Meriwether

Genius's Limits

Investment success accrues not so much to the brilliant as to the disciplined.

　　　　　　　　　　　　　　　　　　　—William Bernstein

Isaac Newton advanced science and thinking like few others ever have. With an IQ of 190, and the ability to calculate to the 55th decimal by hand, his intellect towered above Charles Darwin and Stephen Hawking. But powerful as his brain was, it was unable to save him from falling prey to our most basic human instincts, namely, greed and envy.

In 1720, as shares of the South Sea Company began to rise and hysteria swept the streets of London, Newton found himself in a precarious situation. He bought and sold the stock, earning a 100% return on his investment. Except shares of the South Sea Company rose eightfold in under six months, and they did not stop going higher just because he decided to collect his profits. Unable to cope with the feelings of regret, Newton jumped back into the stock with three times the amount of his original purchase. He reentered as shares approached their apex and instead of doubling his money, he would lose nearly all of it. When the bubble burst, it took just four weeks for prices to plummet 75%.

This left Newton despondent, and it is said that he could not stand to hear the words "South Sea" for the rest of his life. He got an expensive lesson in just how far intelligence goes when attempting to turn money into even more money. When asked about the direction of the markets, Newton replied, "I can calculate the motions of the heavenly bodies, but not the madness of the people." Isaac Newton *actually* was one of the smartest people to ever walk the earth, and not even he was able to resist the sight of other people getting rich without him.

One of the problems many investors face is that we all feel we have a little Isaac Newton in us. We all *feel* we're above average. In a classic 1977 study, "Not Can, But Will College Teaching Be Improved," 94% of professors rated themselves above their peer group average.[1] If traders and investors were asked the same question, I would guess that the results would be very similar. You don't have to be Albert Einstein to realize this math doesn't add up. As Charlie Munger once said, "The iron rule of life is that only 20% of people can be in the top fifth."

To be in Mensa, the largest and oldest high IQ society in the world, members must score in the top 2% of any standardized intelligence test. This means that there are between four and five million brilliant adults living in the United States alone that would qualify for this prestigious society. When you go to your computer screen to buy or sell a stock, there are a lot of these super humans waiting to take the other side of your trade. Therefore, a high IQ guarantees you nothing! This is one of the hardest things for newer investors to come to grips with, that markets don't compensate you just for being smart. Raw brainpower is only one prerequisite to even give yourself a chance of having a positive investment experience. Being smart alone does not determine investment results because markets are not linear. Most formulas eventually fail, if they ever even work at all.

The chances of pulling a nine of spades out of a deck of cards is 1 in 52, but there is no way to calculate the odds of a recession given x, y, and z. With risk assets, one plus two doesn't always equal three, and the graveyard of investors is rife with people who thought they could model their way to above average investing results.

Intelligence in investing is not absolute; it's relative. In other words, it doesn't just matter how smart you are, it matters how smart your competition is. Charlie Ellis brilliantly brought this idea to the forefront in a 1975 article, "The Loser's Game." He wrote "Gifted, determined, ambitious professionals have come into investment management in such large numbers during the past 30 years that it may no longer be feasible for any of them to profit from the errors of all the others sufficiently often and by sufficient magnitude to beat market averages."[2] Not only have ambitious professionals come into investment management, they've also brought with them a whole lot of computer power. These machines have permanently changed the investing landscape. A lot of what used to be considered brilliant is now considered to be standard.

In the 1950s, individuals dominated trading. Now institutions – with nearly unlimited resources – make up 90% of daily trading volume. There are 325,000 Bloomberg terminals and 120,000 Chartered Financial Analysts. Technology and the explosion of information have leveled the playing field.

With any activity that involves both skill and luck, as investing clearly does, as skill and intelligence improve, luck or chance plays an increasing role in the outcome. Michael Mauboussin has written about this idea many times, and he calls it the paradox of skill. The takeaway is that there is a lot of skilled market participants; so, intelligence alone is not enough. Other skills are required. Genius and its limitations are exemplified in no better way than by studying John Meriwether and his band of Einsteins at Long-Term Capital Management.

John Meriwether founded Long-Term Capital Management in 1994 and before that he enjoyed a legendary two-decade career as head of the fixed-income arbitrage group and vice chairman at Salomon Brothers. At Salomon, he surrounded himself with some of the brightest minds in the industry.

Michael Lewis, who began his career at Salomon Brothers, wrote in the New *York Times*, "Meriwether was like a gifted editor or a brilliant director: he had a nose for unusual people and the ability to persuade them to run with their talents ... Meriwether had taken it upon himself to set up a sort of underground railroad that ran from the finest graduate finance and math programs directly onto the Salomon trading floor. Robert Merton, the economist who himself would later become a consultant to Salomon Brothers and, later still, a partner at Long-Term Capital, complained that Meriwether was stealing an entire generation of academic talent."[3]

This generation of academic talent included Eric Rosenfeld, an MIT-trained, Harvard Business School assistant professor, and Victor J. Haghani, who received a master's degree in finance from the London School of Economics. Also on his team were Gregory Hawkins, who got a PhD in financial economics from MIT, and Lawrence Hilibrand, who earned two degrees from MIT. In addition to these rock stars, Long-Term also employed David Mullins, former vice chairman of the US Federal Reserve Board. Meriwether's goal was to outsmart everyone, and this advantage persisted for a long time.

His band of wizards would became the most powerful, profitable group inside of Salomon Brothers. In a year in which John Gutfreund, CEO, earned $3.5 million, Meriwether was reportedly paid $89 million.[4] But after a scandal at the Treasury rocked the bank, Meriwether was forced to resign. Shortly thereafter, his loyal protégés would follow.

Meriwether launched Long-Term Capital Management with two giants of financial academia at his side, who would both later become Nobel Laureates. One was Robert Merton, who earned a bachelor of science in engineering mathematics from Columbia University, a master of science from the California Institute of Technology, and his doctorate in economics from MIT. Prior to joining Salomon Brothers, Merton taught at the MIT Sloan School of Management until 1988, before moving to Harvard University. His pedigree was flawless, and the influence Merton had on the world of finance cannot be overstated. Stan Jonas, a derivatives wizard once said, "Most everything else in finance has been a footnote on what Merton did in the 1970s."[5]

Meriwether was also able to recruit Myron Scholes, cocreator of the Black-Scholes option pricing model. Scholes received his MBA and PhD at the University of Chicago Booth School of Business. He then went on to work at the MIT Sloan School of Management before coming back to teach at Chicago. It should be clear by now that the résumés at Long-Term Capital Management were truly second to none. Nothing in finance had ever even come close. In a *Fortune* article, Carol Loomis said, "There may be more IQ points per square foot than in any other institution extant."[6] They were head and shoulders above everyone else and they knew it. Scholes once described themselves as "Not just a fund. We're a financial-technology company."[7]

The minimum investment at LTCM was $10 million and their management fees were 2 and 25, above the standard industry practice of 2 and 20. The high minimum and above average fees did not deter investors. The smartest minds attracted the smartest and biggest clients, "including David Komansky, head of Merrill Lynch; Donald Marron, chief executive of Paine Webber; and James Cayne, chief executive of Bear Stearns."[8] They also took money from giant institutions like the Bank of Taiwan, the Kuwaiti pension fund, and the Hong Kong Land & Development Authority. Even Italy's central bank, which notoriously *did not* invest in hedge funds, forked over $100 million.[9]

Long-Term Capital Management opened their doors in February 1994 with $1.25 billion, the largest hedge fund opening ever up until that point in time. Their performance was strong right out of the gate. In the first 10 months that they were open, they earned 20%.[10] In 1995, the fund returned 43%, and in 1996, they earned 41% in a year in which their profits totaled $2.1 billion:

> To put this number into perspective, this small band of traders, analysts, and researchers, unknown to the general public and employed in the most arcane and esoteric of businesses, earned more that year than McDonald's did selling hamburgers all over the world, more than Merrill Lynch, Disney, Xerox, American Express, Sears, Nike, Lucent, or Gillette—among the best-run companies and best known brands in American business.[11]

Long-Term Capital Management was on a roll indeed. Their returns were high and steady, with their worst losing month being just a 2.9% decline.[12] It seemed too good to be true. In the fall of 1997, Robert Merton and Myron Scholes both were awarded with the Nobel Prize in Economics. Of their achievement, *The Economist* wrote that they had turned "risk management from a guessing game into a science." Their returns continued uninterrupted and they managed to quadruple their capital without having a single losing quarter.[13]

But the good times would not last forever, because on Wall Street, such winning strategies tend to have a short half-life. Big results breeds big envy, and eventually, every trading secret gets out. LTCM's arbitrage strategies were no exception. As Eric Rosenfeld, an LTCM trader, said, "Everyone else started catching up to us. We'd go to put on a trade, but when we started to nibble the opportunity would vanish."[14] Because opportunities were becoming harder to come by, at the end of 1997, after a 25% gain (17% net of fees), they made the decision to return $2.7 billion of capital to their original investors.[15] They returned all the money that had been invested after 1994 as well as all of the investment profits made before that date.[16]

This became problematic because the opportunities they sought were not large to begin with so their strategy required a ton of leverage. But when they returned $2.7 billion, they did not take down their position sizes, so their leverage went from 18:1 to 28:1.[17] According to Loomis, LTCM wasn't planning to make a hefty return, and they believed the risk was low, but their leverage in both the United States and Europe soared. LTCM had about $40 million at stake for every point in volatility the markets moved.[18]

At one point, they had $1.25 trillion in open positions and they were levered 100:1. This leverage would lead to one of the largest disappearing acts of wealth the world has ever seen.

In May 1998, as the spreads between US and international bonds widened more than their models anticipated, Long-Term lost 6.7%, their worst monthly decline up until that point. In June, the fund fell another 10%, and they were staring down the barrel of a 14% decline for the first half of the year. Russia was at the epicenter of Long-Term's downward spiral, and in August 1998, as oil – their main export – fell by one-third and Russian stocks were down by 75% for the year, short-term interest rates skyrocketed to 200%. And then the wheels fell off for Meriwether and his colleagues. All the brains in the world couldn't save them from what was coming.

LTCM took financial science to its extreme – to the outer limits of sanity. They coldly calculated the odds of every wiggle for every position in their portfolio. In August 1998, they calculated that their daily VAR, or value at risk (how much they could lose), was $35 million. August 21,

1998, is the day when their faith should have evaporated, along with the $550 million that they lost.[19] It was the beginning of the end.

By the end of the month, they had lost $1.9 billion, putting the fund down 52% year-to-date. The death spiral was in full effect. "On Thursday September 10, the firm had lost $530 million; on Friday, $120 million. The next week it hadn't stopped: on Monday, Long-Term dropped $55 million; on Tuesday, $87 million. Wednesday, September 16, was especially bad: $122 million. Like a biblical plague, the losses gave no respite."[20] On Monday, September 21, they lost $553 million.[21]

In the end, in an effort to prevent their failed positions from poisoning the entire financial system, the Federal Reserve Bank of New York would orchestrate a 90%, $3.6 billion takeover, led by 14 Wall Street banks. The fall of Long-Term Capital Management was on a scale the industry had never before witnessed. It was two and a half times as big as Fidelity's Magellan Fund, and four times as big as the next largest hedge fund.[22] Their fund had $3.6 billion in capital, of which two-fifths was personally theirs. In five weeks, it was gone.

How could smart people possibly be so stupid? Their biggest mistake was trusting that their models could capture how humans would behave when money and serotonin are simultaneously exploding. Peter Rosenthal, Long-Term's press spokesman once said, "Risk is a function of volatility. These things are quantifiable."[23] There is a lot of truth in this; after all, at their peak in April 1998, $1 invested turned into $2.85, a 185% profit in just 50 months! But Nassim Taleb, in *Fooled by Randomness*, was also right when he said, "They made absolutely no allowance in the episode of LTCM for the possibility of their not understanding markets and their methods being wrong."[24]

Jim Cramer said, "In short, this was a seminal blowup. It struck at the heart of all of those on Wall Street who think that this racket is a science that can be measured, structured, derived and gamed."[25]

They were able to calculate the odds of everything, but they understood the possibility of nothing. The lesson us mere mortals can learn from this seminal blowup is obvious: Intelligence combined with overconfidence is a dangerous recipe when it comes to the markets.

Notes

1. Patricia K. Cross, "Not Can, But Will College Teaching Be Improved?," *New Directions for Higher Education* 17 (1977): 1–15.

2. Charles D. Ellis, "The Loser's Game," *Financial Analysts Journal* 31, no. 4 (July/August 1975): 19–26.
3. Michael Lewis, "How the Eggheads Cracked," *New York Times Magazine*, January 24, 1999.
4. Janet Lowe, *Damn Right! Behind the Scenes with Berkshire Hathaway Billionaire Charlie Munger* (New York: Wiley, 2000), 194.
5. Roger Lowenstein, *When Genius Failed* (New York: Random House, 2000, 29.
6. Carol Loomis, "A House Built on Sand," *Fortune*, October 26, 1998.
7. Lowenstein, *When Genius Failed*, 65.
8. Edward Chancellor, *Devil Take the Hindmost* (New York: Penguin, 1999), 339.
9. Lowenstein, *When Genius Failed*.
10. Loomis, "A House Built on Sand."
11. Lowenstein, *When Genius Failed*, 94.
12. Ibid., 127.
13. Roger Lowenstein, "Long-Term Capital Management: It's a Short-Term Memory," *New York Times*, September 7, 2008.
14. Lewis, "How the Eggheads Cracked."
15. Chancellor, *Devil Take the Hindmost*, 339.
16. Peter Truell, "Fallen Star Manager," *New York Times*, September 9, 1998.
17. Lowenstein, *When Genius Failed*, 120.
18. Ibid., 126.
19. Lowenstein, "Long-Term Capital Management."
20. Lowenstein, *When Genius Failed*, 180.
21. Ibid., 192.
22. Ibid., 80.
23. Quoted in Lowenstein, *When Genius Failed*, 64.
24. Nassim Taleb, *Fooled by Randomness* (New York: Random House, 2004), 242.
25. Jim Cramer, "Einstein Has Left the Building," TheStreet.com, September 3, 1998.

CHAPTER 5

Jack Bogle

Find What Works for You

> Sometimes in life, we make the greatest forward progress by going backward.
>
> —Jack Bogle

The Vanguard 500 Index fund is the world's largest mutual fund, with $292 billion in assets. That's 292 followed by nine zeros. How do you get to be so gigantic? Start with $11 million and grow 29% per year for the past 40 years. To give you an idea of how much money $292 billion is, if you were to stack it in hundred dollar bills, it would stretch 198 miles, which is just about the round-trip distance from New York City to Vanguard's headquarters in Valley Forge, Pennsylvania.

Index funds have picked up incredible momentum in the past few years. Since the end of 2006, active investors have pulled $1.2 trillion from active mutual funds and plowed $1.4 trillion into index funds.[1] Vanguard has been the biggest beneficiary of the tidal wave of change of investor preference. The only mutually owned mutual fund structure in the world, Vanguard had the largest sales ever by a fund company in 2014, in 2015, and again in 2016.[2] But despite the ubiquity of index funds today, it was not always this way. The idea that investors should settle for "average" returns was once heresy and these funds were often referred to as Bogle's folly.

The effect that Jack Bogle has had on the mutual fund industry and on all of finance cannot be overstated. Vanguard is now ubiquitous, managing more than $4 trillion in client assets. But the idea of capturing "just" market returns, however, was not something that took off right away. In fact, the index fund was met with resentment from the investment community and apathy from investors. The goal for Vanguard's underwriting of the First Index Trust in 1976 was $150 million. When all was said and done, they raised just $11.3 million, a 93% shortfall from their desired target.[3]

The lesson we can learn from one of the most influential investors of all-time is that investing is a long journey, often lasting a lifetime. It is filled with success, failure, hopes, dreams and everything in-between. Jack Bogle is on the Mount Rushmore of investing, and what he will be remembered for, the index fund, was something that he didn't create until three years shy of his 50th birthday!

Twenty-five years before the index fund was created, in his 1951 thesis at Princeton University, Bogle wrote mutual funds "should make no claim to superiority over the market averages." He studied the recent performance of mutual funds and discovered that they trailed the index by 1.6% each year. Later that year, Walter Morgan, a Princeton alum and the founder of the Wellington Fund, hired him. Morgan created one of the first actively managed balanced mutual funds in 1928, with $100,000 (originally under the name The Industrial and Power Securities Company). Almost 90 years later, it is the oldest balanced fund in the United States. The Wellington Fund was one of the few funds to survive the Great Depression, which it owes to the prudence of its founder. The fund had 38% of its assets in cash heading into the crash of 1929. Viewed as a responsible steward of capital, Wellington would gain momentum throughout the Great Depression as many of its competitors fell by the wayside.

When Bogle was hired in 1951, the Wellington Fund managed $140 million. Today, at $95 billion, its assets have grown by 95,000,000%, or just under 17% a year for the past 89 years. But the journey between then and now was hardly a smooth ride.

In 1964, just before its assets would peak at $2 billion, Walter Morgan said, "The name Wellington had a magical ring, a sort of indefinable air of quality about it that made it almost perfect as a name for a conservative financial organization." The conservative financial organization would quickly lose its way. Performance sputtered, the dividend declined, and fund assets cratered to $470 million, a 75% collapse![4]

The fall from grace happened under Bogle's watch. He was a member of the investment committee from 1960 to 1966, and in 1965, at just 36 years old, he was handpicked by Morgan to succeed him as the president of the Wellington Group and in 1970, he was named CEO.

Performance first started to fall behind as Bogle's responsibilities grew. From 1963 to 1966, the flagship Wellington Fund gained just 5.1% annually, well below the 9.3% return of the average balanced fund.[5] As the environment started to heat up and the conservative nature of Wall Street was transformed by the first generation of new blood to enter since the 1920s, management decided it needed to do something to keep up with the changing times. "Lured by the siren song of the Go-Go years, I too mindlessly jumped on the bandwagon."[6]

Their decision to keep up with the times led them to merge with a young Boston firm, Thorndike, Doran, Paine & Lewis Inc. Bogle said the move was designed to achieve three goals:

1. Bring in managers from the "new era" who could return their performance into top results

2. Bring a new speculative growth fund (Ivest Fund) under the Wellington banner.
3. They wanted to gain access into the "rapidly growing investment counseling business."[7]

The merger of these two companies was an odd pairing; it would be like Vanguard purchasing a crypto-currency trading firm today. The following is an excerpt from *The Whiz Kids Take Over*, an article that appeared in *Institutional Investor* in 1968: "Wellington was founded in 1928 with a balanced portfolio of common and preferred stocks and high-grade bonds, with the objective of providing investors with stability, income, and a little low-risk growth to keep pace with inflation … Ivest, on the other hand, was established in 1961, in effect, to make the most of those very fluctuations that Wellington was originally designed to minimize."[8]

The merger turned the Wellington Fund into the antithesis of what led to its long-standing success. From 1929 to 1965, Wellington's equity ratio averaged 62% and its beta averaged 0.6.[9] But with the new kids in town, turnover went from 15% in 1966 to 25% the next year, and stocks, which averaged 55% for a balanced fund, approached 80%.

Shortly after the merger, Bogle was feeling pretty smart about their shrewd business decision. In a recent interview, he said, "The first five years you would have described Bogle as a genius. And at the end of the first 10 years, roughly, you would have said: the worst merger in history, including AOL and Time Warner. It all fell apart. Their management skills were zero. They ruined the fund they started, Ivest. They started two more and ruined both. And they ruined Wellington Fund."[10]

Like so many other funds, Wellington got seduced and ultimately chewed up and spit out by the go-go years of the 1960s:

> The term "go-go" came to designate a method of operating in the stock market – a method that was, to be sure, free, fast, and lively, and certainly in some cases attended by joy, merriment and hubbub. The method was characterized by rapid in-and-out trading of huge blocks of stock, with an eye to large profits taken very quickly, and the term was used specifically to apply to the operation of certain mutual funds, none of which had previously operated in anything like such a free, fast, or lively manner.[11]

Investors found out how their "balanced fund" would be transformed into something completely unrecognizable in the 1967 annual report. Walter Cabot, the new portfolio manager, wrote:

> Times change. We decided we too should change to bring the portfolio more into line with modern concepts and opportunities. We have chosen "dynamic conservatism" as our philosophy, with emphasis on companies that demonstrate the ability to meet, shape and profit from change. [We have] increased our stock position from 64 percent of resources to 72 percent, with a definite emphasis on growth stocks and a reduction in traditional basic industries.... A strong offense is the best defense.[12]

This was written as the go-go years were approaching their apex, the timing could not have been worse. John Dennis Brown, author of *101 Years on Wall Street*, described 1968 as "the most speculative year since 1929."

The go-go years came to a bloody ending in 1969, with the Dow falling 36% in 18 months and individual issues falling much farther. But the stock market bounced back, and the bloody memories were quickly erased in investors' minds. The next things to take hold on Wall Street were the nifty fifty and the "one-decision" stocks. Portfolio managers would no longer rapidly trade these growth stocks, instead they would invest in blue chips like IBM and Disney, and no price was too rich.

But when the air came out of the stock market, they learned the meaning of not confusing brains with a bull market. "The merger that I sought and accomplished not only failed to solve Wellington's problems, it exacerbated them."[13] Ivest, which is one of the reasons they sought TDP&L, lost 55% of its value, compared with a decline of 31% for the S&P 500 over the same time. But the carnage wasn't just limited to Ivest. They had started a few other funds, but they were no better off. When the markets tanked, all of them dropped far below the S&P 500. The Explorer Fund was down 52%, the Morgan Growth Fund slid 47%, and Trustees Equity Fund was down 47%. By 1978, the Trustees Equity Fund had folded and, as Bogle noted, "a speculative fund – Technivest – that we designed to 'take advantage of technical analysis' (I'm not kidding) folded even earlier."[14] You read that right, Jack Bogle, the creator of the index fund, was the CEO of a company that ran a strategy based on technical analysis.

Of all the damage that would be done, the one that cut the deepest was inflicted on their crown jewel, the Wellington Fund. It lost 40%, which was 80% of the decline in the S&P 500. Bogle described this as a "shocking excess relative to Wellington's long history. The loss would not be recouped until 1983, 11 long years later. The 'strong offense' proved no 'defense' at all."[15] The incredible track record and reputation they had built over the years was in jeopardy. The average balanced fund gained 23% for the decade, while Wellington's total return (including dividends) was just 2%.[16]

Bogle looks back on this period of his career with disgust. "I can hardly find words to describe first my regret and then my anger at myself for having made so many bad choices. Associating myself – and the firm whose leadership I had been entrusted – with a group of go-go managers."[17] The blame for the disastrous performance fell on Bogle. He was fired as CEO of Wellington Management in 1974 but convinced the board to let him stay on as chairman and president of the Wellington Fund.

Abject failure would give birth to the most important financial innovation the world has ever seen, the index fund. In 2005, at a Boston Security Analysis Society event, the great Paul Samuelson said:

> I rank this Bogle invention along with the invention of the wheel, the alphabet, Gutenberg printing, and wine and cheese: a mutual fund that never made Bogle rich but elevated the long-term returns of the mutual-fund owners. Something new under the sun.[18]

Bogle had taken all of the lessons he learned and focused his attention into a better way of doing business. By September 1974, he and his team had completed months of research. He was able to bring that to the directors of the funds and convince them to form the Wellington Group, a specialized staff dedicated to Wellington and seven other selected funds. The eight Wellington funds were wholly owned by the funds themselves, "operating on an at-cost basis- a truly *mutual* mutual funds structure, without precedent in the mutual fund industry. The name I chose for the new firm was The Vanguard Group Inc. On September 24, 1974, *Vanguard* was born."[19]

After 16 months of trying to convince the board to create an index fund, the First Index Investment Trust was born. Bogle had shown them the evidence, that over the previous three decades, the S&P 500 index averaged 11.3% growth per year, while the funds trying to beat it earned just 9.7%. The rest is history. Well, sort of. Wall Street wasn't ready to embrace the index fund or stocks for that matter. When they launched in August 1976, stocks were just wrapping up a lost decade. They were trading at the same levels as they had 10 years ago and just experienced the worst bear market since the Great Depression. But determined and sure that he was onto something, Bogle pressed on. He knew that the index fund would give investors their best chance at capturing their fair share of market returns over the long-term.

The First Index Investment Trust did well in its first decade, growing to $600 million (which represented less than one half of 1% of mutual fund assets). But competition was slow to encroach on their territory. In fact, the second index fund wasn't created until 1984, by Wells Fargo. The Stagecoach Corporate Stock Fund came with a 4.5% sales load and an annual expense ratio of 1%.[20] Today, the fund has just $2 billion. I guess there is something to Bogle's saying "ideas are a dime a dozen, but implementation is everything."

Success found its way to index funds in the second decade after their creation, when they went from $600 million to $91 billion. In the end, Bogle was vindicated, and then some.

From 1976 to 2012, the Vanguard 500 returned 10.4%, compared to the 9.2% return of the average large-cap blend funds. The 1.2% difference is nearly identical to the one Bogle presented to his board 40 years earlier. That decades-long track record illustrates the consistent returns that index funds can offer – their primary benefit over other types of investments. Today, index funds represent around 30% of all assets held in mutual funds.

Perhaps most remarkable of all, in 2016, the $289 billion net flows into Vanguard exceeded the other 4,000 global fund providers in Morningstar's database, combined.[21]

Jack Bogle didn't create the index fund until he was 47 years old. So if you've yet to find a method of investing that you're comfortable with, it's not too late! Maybe you've been going back and forth between picking stocks, buying options, or timing the market, all with little to show for it. That's fine, you're still on the path to discovery. I know all about it.

It took me around five years and nearly $20,000 in commissions to realize that I was not destined to be the next Paul Tudor Jones. I was too emotional to be a successful trader, which led me into the arms of Bogle's index funds. Not everybody can buy and hold an index fund – it can be grueling and difficult, rife with drawdowns and potentially decades with nothing to show for it. But warts and all, for me, this is the best way. Not everybody comes to this conclusion and that's okay. The important part is finding a methodology that you are comfortable with. But a methodology means something that is repeatable. It means having a process. The stock market throws far too many curve balls for you to wing it.

With people living longer than ever, we need to expect and be prepared to fund a long retirement. In order to do this, you, like Bogle, need to find what works for you! Hopefully, after reading how a giant like Bogle was dealt a few blows, you'll realize that investing is a lifelong journey of self-discovery. If you're still on your journey, keep searching.

Notes

1. Credit Suisse, "Looking for Easy Games," January 4, 2017.
2. Morningstar, "Recommendations for Fund Companies Not Named Vanguard," December 27, 2016.
3. John C. Bogle, "The Professor, the Student, and the Index Fund," johncbogle.com, September 4, 2011.
4. Vanguard, "Reflections on Wellington Fund's 75th Birthday," 2006.
5. Ibid.
6. Adam Smith, *Supermoney*, foreword by John C. Bogle (Hoboken, NJ: Wiley, 2007).
7. John C. Bogle, *The Clash of the Cultures* (Hoboken, NJ: Wiley, 2012).
8. *Institutional Investor*, "The Whiz Kids Take Over," January 1968.
9. Bogle, *The Clash of the Cultures*, 262.
10. Michael Regan, "Q&A with Jack Bogle: 'We're in the Middle of a Revolution,'" Bloomberg.com, November 23, 2016.
11. John Brooks, *The Go-Go Years* (Hoboken, NJ: Wiley, 1999), 128.
12. Bogle, *The Clash of the Cultures*, 272.
13. Smith, *Supermoney*.
14. Ibid.
15. Bogle, *The Clash of the Cultures*, 272.
16. Smith.
17. Ibid.
18. Quoted in John C. Bogle, "Lightning Strikes," *Institutional Investor* 40, no. 5 (Special 40th Anniversary Issue, 2014): 42–59.
19. Bogle, *The Clash of the Cultures*, 278.
20. Ibid.
21. Ali Masarwah. "Indexing, Vanguard Drove Global Fund Flows," Morningstar.com, February 4, 2017.

CHAPTER 6

Michael Steinhardt

Stay in Your Lane

Investors who confine themselves to what they know, as difficult as that may be, have a considerable advantage over everyone else.
										—Seth Klarman

Making money in the markets is challenging even when you have a deep understanding of what it is that you're doing. Consider specialized professional financial analysts, for example, who have expertise in one particular industry. Even *they* often have a difficult time separating the winners from the losers.

With the proliferation of exchange-traded funds (ETFs) and exchange-traded notes (ETNs), different parts of the market have become more accessible than ever. But just because we *can* trade commodities, currencies, volatility, stocks, and bonds doesn't mean we *should*. Wandering outside of your comfort zone can be a very expensive journey. You don't see lawyers performing oral surgery or accountants drawing blueprints. Similarly, it is your job as an investor to define your circle of competence and stay within that circle.

Warren Buffett is an example of an investor who was deeply intimate with the limitations of his abilities. As the tech bubble inflated in the late 1990s, he was one of the few high-profile investors who never bought into the hype. He knew nothing about semiconductors and even less about the Internet – and he wasn't afraid to admit it. So while shares in his company, Berkshire Hathaway, were cut in half, he stayed true to himself. Buffett never stopped attempting to buy companies that did business in areas he understood. But perhaps more importantly, he never tried to buy a company he couldn't understand, and, as a result, he never paid a ridiculously inflated price.

In July 1999 while at the Sun Valley Conference in Idaho, Buffett got on stage and poured cold water on the current investing landscape. What made this interesting was not that he spoke about the overall market, which he rarely does, but rather whom he was speaking to. Sitting in the audience were Bill Gates, Andy Grove, and other newly minted tech-made millionaires. To them, Buffett's shade looked like nothing more than sour grapes from an old man who couldn't adjust to the times. Over the prior 12 months, Berkshire Hathaway lost 12% of its value, while the NASDAQ 100, a tech-heavy index, rose 74%. Individual tech stocks performed even better over that time; Cisco gained 110%, Yahoo! gained 350%, and Qualcomm gained 408%.

The late nineties were a rough period for value investors. The Internet bubble temporarily changed the way that businesses were valued. For example, eToys Inc. rose 325% on the day of its IPO. At the time, Toys"R"Us was generating 150 times as much revenue and earned $132 million over the previous 12 months, while eToys had lost $73 million. Despite this, eToys was valued at $7.7 billion, while the brick-and-mortar retailer was worth just $5.7 billion.

Stocks like Coca-Cola, Gillette, and the *Washington Post* (Berkshire holdings) were left in the dust as investors dumped value and piled into growth stocks. From peak to trough (June 1998 through March 2000), Warren Buffett's Berkshire Hathaway fell 51% in value! During this time, I estimated that Buffett's net worth fell by more than $10 billion. How much Berkshire did Buffett sell? How much Cisco did he buy? Zero point zero. Not tempted by tech stocks, Buffett remained committed to value investing, and it paid off.[1]

One of the keys to successfully managing your money is to accept, like Buffett did, that there will be times when your style is out of favor or when your portfolio hits a rough patch. It's when you start to reach for opportunities that you can do serious damage to your financial well-being. Michael Steinhardt and his investors learned this lesson in 1994.

Michael Steinhardt is one of those people who was born to pick stocks. There are many mythical stories about investors starting young but Steinhardt *actually* began investing with his bar mitzvah money. His father bought him shares of Penn Dixie Cement and Columbia Gas System. In his autobiography, *No Bull*, he talks about how his interest in stock investing began when he was 13 years old. His entire education and career had been focused on US stocks.[2] Steinhardt's love affair with the stock market would only intensify with the passage of time. He went through his portfolio six times every day, and his obsession paid off, filling his clients' pockets.[3]

Steinhardt was an early pioneer in the hedge fund business and, along with George Soros and Julian Robertson, was one of the big three of the industry. Steinhardt, Fine, Berkowitz & Company opened their doors on July 10, 1967, with $7.7 million. From its inception until he retired in 1995, they returned an average of 24.5% annually, even after taking 20% of the profits. One dollar invested in the fund in 1967 would have been worth $481 on the day he closed the firm in 1995. To underscore how impressive his firm's performance was consider that $1 invested in the S&P 500 would have been worth $19 over the same time period. Stated differently, $10,000 invested with Steinhardt in 1967 would have been worth $4.8 million in 1995 versus the $190,000 it would be worth if it had been invested in the index. These incredible performance numbers are not just abstract. There are a lot of managers with a great, long-term track record that were not able to keep their clients invested through the ups and downs.

Steinhardt once told a story about an early investor who stayed with him through thick and thin and that commitment earned the steadfast client a fortune. The man's name was Richard Cooper, and he first started working with Steinhardt around 1967. His initial investment of $500,000 was worth more than $100 million by the time the firm closed.[4]

Despite his steady performance, Steinhardt was an aggressive trader with unbridled emotions. He recounts the story of learning that one of his firm's portfolios, the only one that was supposed to be low risk, contained bonds that were mismarked. In dressing down the portfolio manager, Steinhardt let loose. He writes, "My rage was uncontrollable. The shouting emanating from my office reached a new decibel level. When the portfolio manager finally had the courage to mutter a few words back to me, he said, 'All I want to do is kill myself.' I replied coolly, 'Can I watch?'"[5] Steinhardt was aware of his tyrannical behavior, but he didn't do much to change it. On top of his temper, he could also be incredibly arrogant, especially when things were going well.

His fiery passion for the stock market enabled him to thrive in almost all market environments throughout his three-decade career, even if his peers were not. In May 1971, *Fortune* ran an article titled "Hedge Fund Miseries" that referenced an SEC study of the destruction that occurred in these funds when the go-go years of the late 1960s came to a screeching halt. Once the bull market slowed, many hedge funds had trouble beating market averages. According to *Fortune*, "The [SEC] study shows that assets of the twenty-eight largest hedge funds – which accounted for 82 percent of the total in 1968 – declined by a whopping 70 percent, or by about $750 million between the end of 1968 and September 30, 1970.... At least one fund showed portfolio gains for the period. Not surprisingly, it emerged as the largest on the SEC's 1970 list. That fund is Steinhardt, Fine, Berkowitz & Co."[6]

Despite Michael Steinhardt's amazing performance record, he, like every single person who has ever put a dollar into the market, experienced agonizing periods. The fund got annihilated in the crash of 1987, and he compounded his problems by buying more S&P index futures on the morning of October 19, 1987. It was a big loss but not a big deal. Most people didn't see the crash coming, although Steinhardt claims he did, but stayed invested anyway. But under his leadership, the firm made it through. What happened next offers investors the most important lesson they can learn from Michael Steinhardt.

In the mid-1990s, hedge fund popularity exploded and investors were knocking down managers' doors to get them to take their money. Steinhardt described the times in *No Bull*:

> It seemed that every "sophisticated" investor wanted to participate in hedge funds, perhaps because their cachet denoted a peculiar exclusivity. Hedge funds became a buzz word. Our firm was bombarded by potential investors who were begging us to let them invest. I could not attend a social event without being besieged with requests to take money from potential investors.[7]

While easy money was available, Steinhardt started his fourth fund (his second offshore) in 1993, the Steinhardt Overseas Fund. They were managing just shy of $5 billion, which was an enormous amount of money back then and still is now. But this big capital base did not come without a cost. He was now responsible for more than 200 times the amount of money he started with, even after adjusting for inflation. It was getting more and more difficult for small and midcap stocks, his bread and butter, to move the needle. So he did something very foolish. He started globetrotting like he was George Soros, and he entered, what was for him, uncharted territory.

Steinhardt was used to the rapid-fire trading of US stocks, but his newfound size became the enemy of performance. It forced him to venture off into areas where he had no expertise. French bonds have as much in common with General Electric stock as an iPhone does with a squirrel. Much of Steinhardt's success had come from his deep understanding of the markets he was trading. Now, he was tempted by potential up-and-comers in emerging markets where he knew little about the business environment and political system. In his memoir he recalls, "Unfortunately, we walked forward unafraid."[8]

Foreign stocks are a few miles outside his circle of competence, but now he was about to travel to the moon. The fund was using swaps and making directional bets on the debt of Europe, Australia, and Japan. Thanks to a barrage of currency cross-trades, the fund's daily profit-and-loss statement had reached 30 pages and was practically indecipherable.

Steinhardt was feeling more brazen about his investing acumen, and his investors would pay for his hubris. Charlie Munger once said, "If you play games where other people have the aptitudes and you don't, you're going to lose." Steinhardt was playing a game that was destined for failure. He had built his success on equity block trading and, as his reputation developed, so did his relationships with the brokers. The sheer size of his firm gave him an edge. As a VIP client, he could always get in touch with someone if he needed to buy or sell quickly. But in Europe, Steinhardt didn't have close, long-term relationships with brokers, so he wasn't at the top of their list when things got hairy. And they were about to get hairy.

Overconfidence drove them to grow much more quickly than was prudent. Steinhardt had no expertise in these markets, but he believed he could apply his deep knowledge of US stocks to find success across the globe. That was a mistake.

Trouble arrived on February 4, 1994, when the Federal Reserve raised interest rates one quarter of 1%. US bonds fell but not nearly as much as European bonds. The bond market meltdown left a hole the size of Europe in Steinhardt's portfolio. He lost $800 million in four days after the rate hikes. For every hundredth of a basis point, he lost $7 million.[9]

Putting too much money into something you don't fully understand is a good way to lose a lot of money. But what's more damaging than losing money is the psychological scar tissue that remains after the money vanishes. His decision to exit his circle of competence sealed his fate. The episode from 1994 left Steinhardt mentally drained. Those feelings could not be shrugged off any longer. In his own words: "1987 had shaken me; 1994 had been devastating. It had taken a part of me that could not be retrieved."[10]

Steinhardt and his clients, the ones who had stayed with him anyway, enjoyed a nice comeback in 1995, as they gained 26% and recouped much of the losses from the previous year. On the back of this rebound, he decided to retire for good at 54 years old.

"Until 1994, he had an unblemished 26-year career as a money manager, giving his investors an average annual return of 31 percent. The Steinhardt funds stumbled badly last year, losing 29 percent, largely by loading up on European bonds whose value plummeted. Assets under management shrank to $2.1 billion at the beginning of this year from about $5 billion at the start of 1994."[11]

Despite the 29% loss in 1994, Steinhardt was able to stitch together one of the most remarkable 30-year track records the industry has seen and ever will see. But for the rest of us, building a successful long-term investment program does not require mind-bending performance. We can't control the returns that the market will give us, but if we can keep our eye on the ball and avoid big errors, we're halfway home.

The temptation to veer off your path never disappears because there is always something going up that you wish you owned, and something going south that you wish you didn't own. For example in 2008 when US stocks fell nearly 40%, long-term US government bonds were up 26%. This is why the behavior gap, the idea that investors underperform not only the market but also their own investments, can shrink but will never fully close. Here's a good example of this; Since March 2009 to August 2016, investors in the largest S&P 500 ETF, SPY, have underperformed the fund by 115%![12]

Bad behavior is one of the greatest dangers investors face, and traveling outside your circle of competence is one of the most common ways that investors misbehave. It's not important how wide your circle of competence is, but what is critically important is that you stay inside it. Knowing what you don't know and having a little discipline can make all the difference in the world.

This isn't to say you should never venture outside your comfort zone, after all, if you never expand your horizons, you'll never learn. But if you are going to invest in areas that you're less familiar with, read the fine print, keep your investments small at first, and limit your losses to fight another day.

Notes

1. Alice Schroeder, *The Snowball* (New York: Bantam, 2009), 31.
2. Michael Steinhardt, *No Bull: My Life In and Out of Markets* (Hoboken, NJ: Wiley, 2004), 5.
3. Ibid., 199.
4. Ibid., 243.
5. Ibid., 179.
6. Wyndham Robertson, "Hedge Fund Miseries," *Fortune*, May 1971, 269.
7. Steinhardt, *No Bull*, 221.
8. Ibid., 222.

9. Roger Lowenstein, *When Genius Failed* (New York: Random House, 2000), 41.

10. Steinhardt, *No Bull*, 238.

11. Stephanie Strom, "Top Manager to Close Shop on Hedge Funds," *New York Times*, October 12, 1995.

12. Michael Batnick, "Distractions Cost Investors 115%," *The Irrelevant Investor*, August 10, 2016.

CHAPTER 7

Jerry Tsai

You're Not as Smart as You Think

> Genius is a rising market.
>
> —John Kenneth Galbraith

Stocks go up most of the time. At least they have historically in the United States. Since 1900, the Dow Jones Industrial Average has experienced double-digit gains in 47% of all years. With the wind often at our back, it's the natural tendency of investors to attribute their gains to skill rather than to favorable market conditions.

Humphrey B. Neill, author of *The Art of Contrary Thinking*, said it best: "Don't confuse brains with a bull market." The idea that we confuse our ability to select above-average stocks in a market that lifts all boats is so pervasive that there's a name for it, attribution bias. "Attribution bias refers to the tendency of people to attribute their successes to their own ability and their failures to external 'unlucky' forces."

A 2013 research paper finds that bull markets lead individual investors to make more trades.[1] The reason we trade more in an environment where we should trade less is because, in a rising market, we constantly receive positive feedback, and we get hooked on the natural stimulants that our bodies produce. To keep this feeling going, we trade more and more, faster and faster. Unfortunately, it's been well documented that turnover and excess returns are negatively correlated. A bull market leaves plenty of margin for error, but when it ends and the tide goes out, we find out who was swimming naked, confusing brains with a bull market.

The Dow Jones Industrial Average peaked in 1929 and the nearly 90% crash that it experienced over the next three years required an 825% increase to get back to even. It took 25 years for the index to traverse that mountain and the industrials eclipsed their previous peak in November 1954, the same year that John Kenneth Galbraith published *The Great Crash*, the quintessential book about the market event that triggered the Great Depression.

The Dow rose from 200 to 680 in the 1950s, a 13% annual increase. The S&P 500 annualized real return (inflation adjusted), including dividends, was 16.76%, which is the best calendar decade ever. Despite this remarkable advance, the 1950s are one of the least documented decades for the stock market. So few people were writing about the investment scenery in the 1950s because the crash and subsequent depression wiped out a whole generation of investors.

After a 90% decline from 1929 to 1932, a rebound, and then another 50% decline in 1937, it's understandable that investors were done with stocks. Because there was little demand for these risky pieces of paper, they spent nearly 50% of the 1940s trading at single-digit price-to-earnings ratios (the long-term average is ~17).

It wasn't just individual investors who wanted little to do with the market, but the financial industry was void of new blood. Between 1930 and 1951, only eight people were hired to work on the New York Stock Exchange trading floor.[2] In *The Money Game*, Adam Smith (a pseudonym for Jerry Goodwyn) wrote, "There is a missing generation on Wall Street, because nobody went there from 1929 to 1947 ... the shadow of deflation hung always over one shoulder; there was always a chance that it might happen again, and this feeling, even unconscious, took a lot of conscious effort to overcome."[3] As Roger Lowenstein put it, "Graham's generation had retired, taking its grim Depression memories with it. Wall Street had reawakened to a younger breed, many of whom had not been alive in 1929, and who were bored with their elders' endless recitations."[4]

By 1969, just 90% of the people employed in the financial industry were over 45 years old.[5] Youth was an enormous asset on Wall Street: "*The Institutional Investor* magazine told of an under-thirty stock analyst with three years' experience and a salary of $25,000, who decided to better his situation by changing jobs. Within two weeks of making known his availability he had fifteen job offers, including one of $30,000 plus bonus and equity in the firm, one of $30,000 with the virtual promise of $50,000 and a partnership in two or three years, and one of $30,000 plus bonus, profit sharing, and deferred compensation."

In 1946, there was only $1.3 billion invested in mutual funds. By 1967, that would multiply many times over, to $35 billion,[6] and money flocked especially to one man, Jerry Tsai. In an era of anonymous money managers, he was the exception.

John Brooks, who wonderfully chronicles the shift from apathy to euphoria in *The Go-Go Years*, wrote, "In the 1920s the man to whom the public ascribed almost supernatural power to divine the future prices of stocks had been Jesse L. Livermore. In the middle 1960s, it was Gerald Tsai."[7]

In 1952, at 24 years old, Jerry Tsai was introduced to Edward Johnson, who ran Fidelity Funds. In 1957, prior to his 30th birthday, Tsai began running the Fidelity Capital Fund. Jerry Tsai was *the* guy, the first celebrity money manager ever. There wasn't a fund manager on the planet who wasn't watching what he was doing. "A number of fund managers I know describe their job very simply, all in nearly the same way. 'My job,' they say, 'is to beat Fidelity.'"[8]

He was trading large blocks of stocks, in and out, rapid-fire. If it was going up faster than the market, he bought it. When it slowed down, he moved onto something else. Another go-go investor, Fred Carr, described this style of trading, "We fall in love with nothing. Every morning everything is for sale – every stock in the portfolio, and my suit and my tie."[9] Edward Johnson described Tsai's style, "It was a beautiful thing to watch his reactions.... What grace, what timing – glorious!" His annual portfolio turnover often exceeded 100%, meaning a share traded for every one held. This was *not* the way Wall Street was used to managing portfolios.[10]

Tsai's timing, grace, and most important, his returns, drew people to the Capital Fund like nothing ever seen before. The number of shareholders rose from 6,200 in May 1960 to 36,000 in May 1961.[11]

Tsai put together an incredible track record with Fidelity. From 1958 to 1965, he returned 296%, compared to a gain of 166% for the average conservative equity fund.[12] But Fidelity was a family-owned company, and despite Tsai's success, and being named an executive vice president in 1963, he was fully aware that Ned Johnson would succeed his father. So in 1965, Tsai sold his stock back to the company for $2.2 million and left Boston for New York to hang his own shingle, launching the Manhattan Fund.

Hailed as a hero, even by competitors, Tsai was recognized as one of the top fund managers on the scene, and he was giving the industry a good name. What his investors, competitors, and even Tsai himself saw as skill and genius was nothing more than luck.

Tsai's Manhattan Fund first planned to offer 2.5 million shares to the public, but investor appetite for the original high-frequency trader was 10 times greater than Tsai had anticipated. They issued 27 million shares and raised $247 million in capital, representing what was at the time the biggest offering ever for an investment company.[13] This extraordinary amount represented nearly 15% of the total cash flow into equity funds that year.[14] Investors were even willing to forfeit 8.5% in the way of a sales load to get access to the most famous money manager of the time. But the bloom would soon come off the rose.

Talking about Jerry Tsai was fashionable, and the Manhattan Fund was a constant topic of conversation. He had a larger-than-life presence on Wall Street. It was hard to keep up with Tsai's lightning-quick moves and what his actual holdings were, but that didn't stop people from making assumptions. Not only did people pay close attention, they both rooted for Tsai and waited for him to get stuck in a position that would send him spiraling downward.[15] And soon, Tsai would quickly go from being on top of the world to buried underneath the scorn of his investors.

In Tsai's go-go years, high-flying stocks with positive momentum were all the rage. Polaroid, Xerox, IBM all traded at price-to-earnings ratios of more than 50. These expensive stocks were supported by explosively high growth rates. From 1964 to 1968, IBM, Polaroid, and Xerox grew their earnings per share at 88%, 22%, and 171%, respectively. Others like University Computing, Mohawk Data, and Fairchild Camera traded at several-hundred times their trailing 12-month earnings. The latter three and many others like them would go on to lose more than 80% in the 1969–1970 bear market.

The Manhattan Fund was up almost 40% in 1967, more than double the Dow. But in 1968, he was down 7% and was ranked 299th out of 305 funds tracked by Arthur Lipper.[16]

When the market crash came, the people responsible were entirely unprepared. By 1969, half of the salesmen on Wall Street had only come into the business since 1962[17] and had seen nothing but a rising market. And when stocks turned, the highfliers that went up the fastest also came down the fastest. For example, National Student Marketing, which Tsai bought 122,000 shares for $5 million, crashed from $143 in December 1969 to $3.50 in July 1970.[18] Between September and November 1929, $30 billion worth of stock value vanished; in the 1969-1970 crash, the loss was $300 billion![19]

The gunslingers of the 1960s were thinking only about return and paid little attention to risk. This carefree attitude was a result of the market they were playing in. From 1950 through the end of 1965, the Dow was within 5% of its highs 66% of the time, and within 10% of its highs 87% of the time. There was virtually no turbulence at all. From 1950 to 1965, the only bear market was "The Kennedy Slide," which chopped 27% off the S&P 500, and recovered in just over a year.

Tsai was playing a game that could not be consistently won. He was the first of a new breed of traders who ditched the slow-and-steady to chase immediate profits. Led by Tsai, the Manhattan Fund was a pioneer of this micro-term strategy – and copycats lined up to mimic their every move. According to Lowenstein, "It was said that a whisper of Tsai's involvement in a stock was sufficient to set off a small stampede."[20]

Tsai saw the writing on the wall, and in August 1968, he sold Tsai Management and Research to C.N.A. Financial Corporation, an insurance company, for stock worth around $30 million.

Looking back on his experience, Tsai was not fond of the way he was treated:

> Nineteen sixty-seven was a very good year for the Manhattan Fund; we were up 58 percent, as I recall. I think among the big funds, we were the best. So I must have been feeling pretty good that year. Not the following year. The following year felt lousy. The stocks that did so well in '67 did not do well in '68. Either I overstayed, or I had the wrong stocks. But I think the press has been very unkind, because Fidelity Capital started in 1958, so you might say, from 1958 to 1967 we were always on top. We had one bad year, in 1968, and I've been killed in the press ever since. Like a ballplayer, right? If you have ten good games and one lousy game, you're a bum. I don't think that's fair.[21]

Tsai did have "ten good games," but the game he was playing was like bowling with bumpers in the gutters. He was throwing the ball as hard as he could, and it was working. But when the bumpers were taken away, in 1968, his investors learned a very hard and important lesson. The Manhattan Fund would lose 90% of its assets over the next few years; by 1974, it had the worst eight-year performance in mutual fund history to date. A rising market lifts all ships, and Tsai's investors learned a very important lesson: Don't confuse brains with a bull market!

Notes

1. Zhen Shi and Na Wang, "Don't Confuse Brains with a Bull Market: Attribution Bias, Overconfidence, and Trading Behavior of Individual Investors," EFA 2010 Frankfurt Meetings paper, September 4, 2013.
2. John Brooks and Michael Lewis, *The Go-Go Years* (Hoboken, NJ: Wiley, 1999), 113.
3. Adam Smith, *The Money Game* (New York: Vintage, 1967), 178.
4. Roger Lowenstein, *Buffett* (New York: Random House, 1995), 96.
5. Brooks and Lewis, *The Go-Go Years*, 211.
6. Smith, *The Money Game*, 180.
7. Brooks and Lewis, *The Go-Go Years*, 5.
8. Smith, *The Money Game*, 23.
9. Lowenstein, *Buffett*, 99.

10. Brooks and Lewis, *The Go-Go Years*, 135.
11. *New York Times*, "Fidelity Capital Shows Wide Gains," July 7, 1961.
12. John C. Bogle, Foreword to *Supermoney* by Adam Smith (Hoboken, NJ: Wiley, 2007).
13. Brian Stelter, "Gerald Tsai, Innovative Investor, Dies at 79," *New York Times*, July 11, 2008.
14. Bogle, *Supermoney*.
15. Smith, *The Money Game*, 202–203.
16. David N. Dremen, *Psychology and the Stock Market* (New York: Amacom, 1977), 84.
17. Brooks and Lewis, *The Go-Go Years*, 162.
18. Dremen, *Psychology and the Stock Market*, 93.
19. Brooks and Lewis, *The Go-Go Years*, 162.
20. Lowenstein, *Buffett*, 99.
21. The Editors of Institutional Investor, *The Way It Was: An Oral History of Finance 1967–1987* (New York: William Morrow & Co., 1988), 138.

CHAPTER 8

Warren Buffett

Beware of Overconfidence

It ain't what you don't know that gets you into trouble. It's what you know for sure that just ain't so.

—Mark Twain

One day in early 2017, $105 billion worth of S&P 500 stocks were traded. Every person that sold and every algorithm that bought thought they were on the right side of the trade. It's true, investors are a confident bunch.

When it comes to the future, which is by definition unpredictable, we tend to believe we know more than we actually can. One of the ways that this manifests itself in investing is in something called the endowment effect. After consumers or investors make a purchase, we value this new possession more than we did before it was ours.

Imagine you're wagering on a football game in which the two teams competing are of no rooting interest to you. It's a coin toss. You go back and forth several times, but finally decide to pull the trigger on the team with the less talented quarterback but a stronger defense. After you've walked to the counter and placed your bet, you'll immediately feel much better about your decision than before you parted with your dollars. Kahneman, Knetsch, and Thaler documented this in an experiment in their 1991 paper, "Anomalies: The Endowment Effect, Loss Aversion, and Status Quo Bias."[1]

In an advanced undergraduate economics class at Cornell, 22 students in alternating seats were given coffee mugs that sell for $6 at the bookstore. When sellers were given the option to sell, and buyers given the option to buy, the study found that the median owner was unwilling to sell for less than $5.25, while the median buyer was unwilling to pay more than $2.25. Once something belongs to us, objective thinking flies out the window.

The main effect of this "endowment," the authors found, "is not to enhance the appeal of the good one owns, only the pain of giving it up." In other words, to go back to the example of the gambler who was tossing a mental coin between two teams, had the gambler been asked if they would like to change their mind, it's highly unlikely they would say yes. Confidence grows exponentially once you've decided on something you were previously unsure about.

Overconfidence is so ingrained in our DNA that even if we're aware of it, shielding ourselves from it becomes supremely difficult. Robert Shiller has written, "Our satisfaction with our views of the world is part of our self-esteem."[2] This applies to everyone, but especially to people in the financial business. David Dreman shows how overconfident financial analysts are in his book, *Contrarian Investment Strategies*:

> Analysts were asked for their high and low estimates of the price of a stock. The high estimate was to be the number they were 95 percent sure the actual price would fall below; the low estimate was the price they were 95 percent sure the stock would remain above. Thus, the high and low estimates should have included 90 percent of the cases, which is to say that if the analysts were realistic and unbiased, the number of price movements above and below the range would be 10 percent. In fact, the estimates missed the range 35 percent of the time, or three and a half times as often as estimated.[3]

It's not just the average Joe investor or even financial professionals that fall victim to this embedded blind spot, it's everyone who has ever bought or sold a stock, including one of the greatest investors of all time, Warren Buffett. The Oracle of Omaha, as he is colloquially known, has the most impressive long-term track record of anybody to ever play the game. Since 1962, when he first purchased stock in Berkshire Hathaway, a small textile manufacturing company in New Bedford, Massachusetts, the Dow Jones Industrial Average is up 30 fold. Berkshire Hathaway is up 33,333 fold.

Buffett took control of Berkshire in 1965, and over that time, it's grown 1,972,595%, or 20.8% annually. To give an idea of what a feat this is, $10,000 compounded at 20.8% for 52 years grows to $185,131,161.

Before he became the company-gobbling, folksy billionaire that we know him as today, this stock-picking wizard ran a limited partnership from 1957 to 1969. In that 12-year stretch, his gross returns were 2,610%, versus 186% for the Dow. His limited partners received 1,400%, or 25%, annually, net of fees! Buffett's investors would receive the first 4% that he could generate, and they would share any remaining profits – 75% to the clients and 25% to Buffett.[4] All of Buffett's net worth was invested alongside them, so to say he ate his own cooking is an understatement. He accomplished this magnificent lifelong track record across more than four decades, regardless of whether the markets were bullish or bearish, through nine presidential administrations and in spite of every economic cycle and groundbreaking technology.

One of the underrated things about Warren Buffett is his ability to communicate his investment philosophy. Before there were blogs and long before the Internet, he was writing client letters, which have become appointment reading for thousands of investors around the globe. While operating the partnership, one of the messages that was repeated over and over was setting a proper benchmark and having realistic expectations. As time went by and his performance got better and better, he warned his partners not to get too confident that he would continue with such spectacular results.

Lowenstein pulled highlights from Buffett's annual forecasts to illustrate how he aimed to temper expectations:

1962: "If my performance is poor, I expect my partners to withdraw."
1963: "It is certainty that we will have years when ... we deserve the tomatoes."
1964: "I believe our margin over the Dow cannot be maintained."
1965: "We do not consider it possible on an extended basis to maintain the 16.6 percentage point advantage over the Dow."
1966: "We are going to have loss years and are going to have years inferior to the Dow – no doubt about it."
July 1966: "Such results should be regarded as decidedly abnormal."[5]

In 1967, he wrote to his clients sentiments that he would echo 30 years later, in the dot-com bubble:

When the game is no longer being played your way, it is only human to say the new approach is all wrong, bound to lead to trouble, etc. I have been scornful of such behavior by others in the past. I have also seen the penalties incurred by those who evaluate conditions as they were – not as they are. Essentially I am out of step with present conditions. On one point, however, I am clear. I will not abandon a previous approach whose logic I understand even though it may mean foregoing large, and apparently easy, profits to embrace an approach which I don't fully understand, have not practiced successfully and which, possibly, could lead to a substantial permanent loss of capital.[6]

Buffett revised his goal of beating the Dow by 10 percentage points to a 9% annual gain, or 5% above the Dow, whichever was lower. And then in 1968, warnings be damned, he returned 58.8%, or 45.6% net of fees. The Dow was up just 7.7% that year. He wrote to his partners that the result "should be treated as a freak – like picking up thirteen spades in a bridge game." In 1969 he had had enough, at just 39 years old, he shut down the partnership, before his warnings ever came to fruition.

It's funny that despite his monstrous returns and his youth, two things that tend to favor the brash, Buffett's confidence level was kept in check. It's funnier still, that at 63, oozing with confidence, he would make the single costliest mistake of his investing career.

The Oracle became the second wealthiest man in the world by buying and holding great businesses.[7] In 1972, after arm wrestling with his partner Charlie Munger over the price, Berkshire Hathaway purchased See's Candy for $30 million. They could have paid multiples of the $25 million Buffett wanted to and done just fine, because See's Candy has generated $1.9 billion pretax since 1972.[8] In 1983, Berkshire bought 90% of Nebraska Furniture Mart, for $55 million. It's now the largest furniture store in the country. In 2011, the company earned 10 times as much as it did when they first purchased it. In 2015, Nebraska Furniture Mart opened a store in Texas, which did $750 million in sales in its first year alone.

Buffett purchased very nice companies in his career, but it wasn't See's or the Furniture Mart that landed him a top the *Forbes* 400; it was insurance.

Buffett took to insurance early. In 1951, while in business school, he took a trip to Washington where the Government Employees Insurance Company, or GEICO, was located. Ben Graham, the dean of security analysis and Buffett's teacher at Columbia, was the chairman of the company. At the time, their sales were $8 million annually. Today, they do that every three hours[9] and own 12% of industry volume. Buffett first bought the stock in 1952 and sold it a year later for a 50% profit.[10]

In 1967, Buffett bought National Indemnity for $8.6 million, and today it's the world's largest property/casualty insurance company. He continued to track GEICO from his days as a business student and when he was finally given a fat pitch, he swung for the fences. In 1976, GEICO announced they lost $126 million in the previous year, and the stock traded down to 4 7/8, after being as high as 42 two years earlier. He bought 500,000 shares and continued to add, quickly becoming a controlling owner.[11] In early 1996, Berkshire bought the remaining half of GEICO that it didn't own for $2.3 billion (he spent just $46 million for the first 48%[12]). Today, GEICO does $462 million in underwriting profit, and has $17 billion in float.

Buffett outlined his interest in GEICO in Berkshire Hathaway's 2016 annual letter. GEICO, like other property/casualty insurers, collects premiums from all clients up front. Then, they pay claims as they are submitted. Buffett explains:

> This collect-now, pay-later model leaves P/C companies holding large sums – money we call 'float' – that will eventually go to others. Meanwhile, insurers get to invest this float for their own benefit. Though individual policies and claims come and go, the amount of float an insurer holds usually remains fairly stable in relation to premium volume.[13]

But not every purchase would be a winner. In 1987, there was the $700 million investment in Salomon Brothers, their biggest investment up until that point, which turned out to be lucrative but was mentally and emotionally depleting, after a scandal with the Treasury was uncovered in 1991.

In 1990, they took a 12% stake in US Air, which eventually would stop paying dividends on preferred shares. Berkshire's stake which was acquired for $358 million, was valued at just $86 million a few years later, a cool 76% decline. Charlie Munger said, "It was a humbling experience. To sit there and watch that net worth melt away – $150 million, $200 million … It worked out fine for Berkshire. But we're not looking for another experience like it."[14]

These less-than-stellar experiences pale in comparison to Buffett's costliest mistake. In 1993, Berkshire agreed to buy Dexter Shoes for $433 million. But it wasn't just that this business would be worth zero a few years later that was the problem, it was the stock that Berkshire issued to pay for it. The shares were trading for $16,765 at the time of the transaction. Today, at $242,000, the 25,200 shares that they exchanged for Dexter have grown 1350%. At the time, Berkshire's market cap was $19 billion. I could only imagine what Buffett would have thought had someone told him the shares he just gave to a business destined for zero would end up being worth $6 billion, one-third of its market cap at the time of this transaction.

Buffett knew what he was doing. This was not his first time buying an entire company – it wasn't even his first time buying a shoe company. In July 1991, Berkshire acquired H. H. Brown, which was the leading

North American manufacturer of work shoes and boots, and had "a history of earning unusually fine margins on sales and assets."[15] So when he had the opportunity to buy Dexter, which made reasonably priced men's and women's shoes, he jumped at it.

Buffett told the *New York Times* that "Dexter Shoe Co. is exactly the type of business Berkshire Hathaway admires … it has a long, profitable history, enduring franchise and superb management."[16]

Berkshire shareholders were told about Dexter in the 1993 annual letter:

> What we did last year was build on our 1991 purchase of H. H. Brown, a superbly-run manufacturer of work shoes, boots and other footwear. Brown has been a real winner: Though we had high hopes to begin with, these expectations have been considerably exceeded thanks to Frank Rooney.... Because of our confidence in Frank's team, we next acquired Lowell Shoe, at the end of 1992. Lowell was a long-established manufacturer of women's and nurses' shoes, but its business needed some fixing. Again, results have surpassed our expectations. So we promptly jumped at the chance last year to acquire Dexter Shoe of Dexter, Maine, which manufactures popular-priced men's and women's shoes. Dexter, I can assure you, needs *no* fixing: It is one of the best-managed companies Charlie and I have seen in our business lifetimes.[17]

Buffett certainly was aware of some of the business challenges Dexter faced, but as Alice Schroeder described in her wonderful biography, *The Snowball*, "Here he was a little outside his 'circle of competence,' making a bet that demand for imported shoes would wane."[18] In looking at the language Buffett used to describe Dexter to his shareholders, it's clear that the whiz-kid investor who warned his investors not to be over-confident had grown into a confident, company-guzzling businessman. Buffett wrote:

> Five years ago we had no thought of getting into shoes. Now we have 7,200 employees in that industry, and I sing "There's No Business Like Shoe Business" as I drive to work.... Finally, and of paramount importance, Harold and Peter can be sure that they will get to run their business – an activity they dearly love – exactly as they did before the merger. At Berkshire, we do not tell .400 hitters how to swing.

In *Charlie Munger: The Complete Investor*, Tren Griffin writes, "In doing their due-diligence analysis for Dexter Shoes, Buffett and Munger made the mistake of not making sure the business had a moat and being too focused on what they thought was an attractive purchase price."[19]

Psychologists Dale Griffin and Amos Tversky wrote, "Intuitive judgments are overly influenced by the degree to which the available evidence is representative of the hypothesis in question."[20] The evidence Buffett had available, other than Dexter's financials and the proposed purchase price, was the success he experienced less than two years earlier with his purchase of H. H. Brown. Buffett did what every person on earth does, he reached for whatever was easiest to remember in deciding whether or not to do something; in the case of buying Dexter's shoes, it was the success of purchasing H. H. Brown.

Buffett was overconfident in Frank Rooney, who headed H. H. Brown and helped broker the Dexter acquisition. Buffett also put too much stock in Harold Alfond, the leader at Dexter. Finally, he had too much confidence in himself. But things would quickly go south at Dexter, and there was no mention of the company in any of Berkshire's letters for the next five years.

Then, troubles started to surface. For five years, starting in 1994, the company's shoe profits and revenues had been in decline. By 1999, revenue had declined by 18% and operating profits were down 57%.[21] In his annual letter that year, Buffett wrote:

> We manufacture shoes primarily in the U.S., and it has become extremely difficult for domestic producers to compete effectively. In 1999, approximately 93% of the 1.3 billion pairs of shoes purchased in this country came from abroad, where extremely low-cost labor is the rule.[22]

By 2000, it was no longer a question of whether he could turn the shoe manufacturer around:

> I clearly made a mistake in paying what I did for Dexter in 1993. Furthermore, I compounded that mistake in a huge way by using Berkshire shares in payment. Last year, to recognize my error, we charged off all the remaining accounting goodwill that was attributable to the Dexter transaction. We may regain some economic goodwill at Dexter in the future, but we clearly have none at present.[23]

Buffett might have been blinded by confidence when he purchased Dexter, but he was quick and forthcoming when acknowledging the mistake. In 2014, he wrote, "As a financial disaster, this one deserves a spot in the *Guinness Book of World Records*."[24]

Buffett devoted more words on the mistake at Dexter in 2007, 2014, and 2016. In fact, one of Buffett's strengths is in recognizing that mistakes are part of the game. Buffett has included the word "mistake" 163 times in his annual letters. He, like everybody else who has ever put a dollar into the market, is no stranger to lousy investments.

Buffett earned the right to be confident, but his overconfidence cost Berkshire Hathaway $6 billion. For the rest of us, it behooves us to take a minute and think about why we're investing and what we *really* know. Do you know more than the person on the other side of the trade? Do you know something that's not in the newspaper or on the Internet? Will we know when we're right? What about if we're wrong? Overconfidence is so ingrained in us that just being aware of it does nothing to prevent it.

Buffett has a great way for investors to deal with overconfidence. If you were given a punch card with just 20 holes, and those represented all the investments you could make for the rest of your life, you would think much more carefully about what you were doing. Now this is not practical advice, in real life nobody is this disciplined, but it's a great way to think about how much thought and care should go into each investment. By taking the time to think something through, we can slow down and suppress impulsive actions. But take too much time, and process too much information, and we're likely to become more confident! It all leads back to thinking we know more than we possibly can, and this is very difficult to overcome.

The best way to guard against overconfidence when making speculative investments is to have a plan ahead of time. Know when you're wrong; use price levels, dollar loss levels, or percentage loss levels. Making decisions ahead of time, especially decisions that involve admitting defeat, can help conquer one of the biggest hurdles investors face; looking in the mirror and seeing an ability that we just do not possess.

Notes

1. Daniel Kahneman, Jack L. Knetsch, and Richard H. Thaler, "Anomalies: The Endowment Effect, Loss Aversion, and Status Quo Bias," *Journal of Economic Perspectives* 5, no. 1 (Winter 1991): 193–206.

2. Robert Shiller, *Irrational Exuberance* (Princeton, NJ: Princeton University Press, 2000), 60.

3. David Dreman, *Contrarian Investment Strategies: The Psychological Edge* (New York: Free Press, 2012), 176.

4. Roger Lowenstein, *Buffett* (New York: Random House, 2008), 62.

5. Ibid., 93.

6. Warren Buffett, Partnership Letter, October 9, 1967.

7. Warren Buffett, 2016 Berkshire Hathaway annual letter, February 25, 2017.

8. Warren Buffett, 2014 Berkshire Hathaway annual letter, February 25, 2015.

9. Buffett, 2016 Berkshire Hathaway annual letter.

10. Lowenstein, *Buffett*, 49.

11. Ibid., 195.

12. Snowball 540.

13. Buffett, 2016 Berkshire Hathaway annual letter.

14. Janet Lowe, *Damn Right! Behind the Scenes with Berkshire Hathaway Billionaire Charlie Mungre* (New York: Wiley, 2000), 183.

15. Warren Buffett, 1991 Berkshire Hathaway annual letter, February 28, 1992.

16. Quoted in *New York Times*, "Company News; Berkshire Hathaway Set to Acquire Dexter Shoe," October 1, 1993.

17. Warren Buffett, 1993 Berkshire Hathaway annual letter, March 1, 1994.

18. Alice Schroeder, *The Snowball* (New York: Bantam, 2009).

19. Tren Griffin, *Charlie Munger: The Complete Investor* (New York: Columbia University Press, 2015).

20. Dale Griffin and Amos Tversky, "The Weighing of Evidence and the Determinants of Confidence," *Cognitive Psychology* 24 (1992): 411–435.

21. Anthony Bianco, "The Warren Buffett You Don't Know," Bloomberg .com, July 5, 1999.

22. Warren Buffett, 1999 Berkshire Hathaway annual letter, March 1, 2000.

23. Warren Buffett, 2000 Berkshire Hathaway annual letter, February 28, 2001.

24. Warren Buffett, 2014 Berkshire Hathaway annual letter, February 25, 2015.

CHAPTER 9

Bill Ackman

Get Off Your Soapbox

> Our satisfaction with our views of the world is part of our self esteem and personal identity.
>
> —Robert Shiller

I once saw the Nobel Prize–winning psychologist Daniel Kahneman say, "Ideas are part of who we are. They become like possessions. Especially publicly. I mean, flip flopping is a bad word. I love changing my mind!" This attitude stands in stark contrast to most investors, who loathe to do few things more than kill a previously held belief. Our inability to process information that challenges our ego is one of the biggest reasons why so many investors fail to capture market returns.

The world is always changing, but our views usually don't evolve alongside it. Even when we're presented with evidence that disconfirms our previous views, straying far from our original feelings is too painful for most to bear. This is so deeply ingrained in the fabric of our DNA that there is a name for this natural mental malfunction; it's called cognitive dissonance. For example, ask anybody if they have the ability to predict the future. They might look at you funny, and say, "Are you asking me if I have a crystal ball? No, I do not." Okay then, do you select individual stocks. And do you regularly buy and sell them, in anticipation that their future price will be higher or lower? These people are paying lip service to the idea that they can't predict the future, because their actions contradict their words.

Investors actively seek out and consume information that makes them feel better about their current opinions. But this type of behavior is not limited to the Average Joe investor. In fact, the more experience you have, the more confident you become, and the less likely you are to accept you're wrong, even when a 50% decline says otherwise.

Human beings are social creatures that love to tell stories, and few things are more conducive to storytelling than investing. The stock market provides us with thousands of different companies to invest in. There are publicly traded businesses that are in oil service fields, grocery stores, transportation, artificial intelligence, pharmaceuticals, leisure, retail, equipment builders, and everything in-between. And the prices are changing every day, providing literally endless material for fodder.

A Fidelity study showed that in social settings, people prefer to share their success rather than their failure. Fifty-nine percent shared their profitable trades with friends and family; only 52% shared their failures.[1] People love sharing their battles on the financial gridiron so much that at one point in 1998, there were 400,000 Americans participating in an investment club. These people would come together occasionally and talk about the stock they bought that doubled since the last meeting, the tiny biotech company that got approval on a new drug, or the technology company that just beat earnings. But the number of people getting together to talk shop has shrunk every year since then, and was less than one-tenth the size by 2012.[2]

The stock market might take the blame for why people no longer meet to discuss their favorite companies. Two 50% declines will crush even the most enthusiastic storytellers. But perhaps there is another reason why people are no longer participating; it's really hard to become a better investor by getting ideas from others. Worse, once you share ideas of your own, hopping off as the story turns south will stifle even the most open-minded, egoless people out there.

Most of the gains in the stock market come from the giant winners. In fact, most stocks downright stink. Four out of every seven common stocks in the United States have underperformed one-month Treasury bills. And because there are so many lousy stocks, there's a high probability that over time, you will be exposed as an ordinary person, possessing no superior stock-picking ability than the person sitting next to you. And being wrong again and again and again is mentally exhausting, especially when it comes to something as personal as money. Investors would be a lot better off financially if they would just keep their personal finances personal. We can learn a lot from somebody who takes the exact opposite approach, who is one of the most vocal and public investors of all time.

Bill Ackman started in the hedge fund world in 1993 at just 26 years old. He and a Harvard Business School classmate, David Berkowitz, with $3 million in capital provided from several investors, started Gotham Partners. They found success early on with classic, old-school value investing. They bought companies for less than they estimated them to be worth, and this helped them turn $3 million into $568 million at their peak in 2000. But they got into trouble, like so many successful investors do, by straying from where their bread was buttered. Ackman's confidence led him to take positions that were unwise, by any objective measure, and he was left holding a roster of unpopular companies that were not in demand. The *New York Times* explained it this way: "An examination of Gotham's activities in recent years shows a series of ill-timed bets, a surprising lack of diversification and a dangerous concentration in illiquid investments that could not easily be sold when investors wanted their money back."[3] So by the end of 2002, they announced their intention to wind down the fund. It was not so much a decision they made, but rather an outcome that was forced on them when investors started asking for their money back in droves.

Bill Ackman wasn't going to let one blown-up hedge fund slow him down. He is one of the most competitive investors the industry has ever seen. Even as a high school student, he was always looking for a challenge. He once bet his father $2,000 that he would get a perfect score on the SAT verbal test. Just before taking the test, his father, convinced his son's goal was impossible, withdrew from the agreement, saving Ackman from a $2,000 loss. He got 780 on the verbal section, "One wrong on the verbal, three wrong on the math," he muses. "I'm still convinced some of the questions were wrong."[4]

After closing Gotham, Ackman eventually got back on the horse. In January 2004, he started a new fund, Pershing Square Capital Management. He began with $10 million of his own money and $50 million raised from a single investor, and would open the fund to outside investors in 2005. The money flooded in, attracting some $220 million.[5]

The new Ackman would no longer invest passively. Gone were the days of buying a company at a discount, and letting the chips fall where they may. Bill Ackman rose from the ashes of Gotham Partners like a phoenix and came out one of the most aggressive activist investors of his era. An activist investor is one who acquires a large enough shares in a company to enact changes. They'll try to persuade management to be more shareholder friendly, which is code for increase the stock price. If they're not successful, they can push for a seat on the board and enact changes from the inside.

Activist investors are a confident bunch. It's one thing to purchase shares in a company, it's another thing entirely to impose your will on a management team and tell them how to run their business. The stakes are high in this arena and when successful, the payoff can be enormous. For example, Ackman took a 10% stake in Wendy's, one of his first targets at Pershing, and they agreed to spin off Tim Hortons.[6] From April 2005 to March 2006, Wendy's stock appreciated by 55%.[7]

In 2005, Ackman targeted McDonald's, proposing they spin-off their low-margin business. He bought 62 million shares and options that, if exercised, would value his stake at $2 billion, one of the largest ever for a hedge fund up until that time.[8] McDonald's had other ideas, saying, "The proposal is an exercise in financial engineering and does not take into account McDonald's unique business model." Ackman said, "Our intention is to change their intention." Ackman is not one to take no for an answer. "I'm the most persistent person you will ever meet."[9]

Other companies that landed in Ackman's crosshairs were MBIA Inc., Target, Sears, Valeant, and J. C. Penney. But perhaps no investor and no company will ever be more joined at the hip than his bet against Herbalife. If you Google "Bill Ackman Herbalife," you get 180,000 results. Ackman's storied battle with the multilevel marketing company has been in the *New York Times* and the *Wall Street Journal* dozens of times, it's been written about in *Fortune*, the *New Yorker*, and *Vanity Fair*.

Joe Nocera wrote about Ackman's long and drawn out battle with MBIA Inc. in the *New York Times*:

> But for sheer, obsessive doggedness, nothing he has ever done can compare with his pursuit of a company called MBIA Inc. In fact, I don't think I've ever seen a fund manager grab a company by the tail and simply not let go the way Mr. Ackman has done with this once-obscure holding company, whose main subsidiary, MBIA Insurance, is the nation's largest bond insurer.[10]

After seven years, Ackman would ultimately be vindicated, and he walked away with $1.4 billion in profits.[11] But his battle with MBIA was a warm-up for the war he would have with Herbalife.

By definition, activist investors are public, because once you acquire 5% of a company, you must file a 13D registration with the Security and Exchange Commission. Short positions, however, do not have to be disclosed, but Ackman chooses to do so anyway, like nobody has ever done before.

Herbalife is a Los Angeles–based company that sells weight loss products and nutritional supplements. Herbalife has been in business for 37 years, and now operates in 90 countries. In its first year, 1980, Herbalife did $23,000 in sales. That grew to $500 million by 1984 and to $1 billion by 1996. In the year before Ackman shorted the company, they did $5.4 billion in sales and had the highest paid CEO in America.

On December 20, 2012, 500 people gathered to watch him deliver his short presentation, "Who Wants to Be a Millionaire?" Ackman accused

Herbalife of being a pyramid scheme, and said he would donate any profits made, "blood money" as he called it, to charity.[12]

Ackman's presentation noted that Herbalife was worth more than Energizer Holdings, The Clorox Company, and Church and Dwight. These consumer companies own Arm & Hammer Baking Soda, Trojan condoms, Energizer batteries, Edge shaving gel, Clorox Wipes, and others that you find in homes all across the United States. Ackman asked the poignant question, "Has anyone ever purchased an Herbalife product?"

A key distinction between these companies was their gross margins, meaning their profits once you remove the cost of goods sold. The three traditional companies made between 42% and 46% on their products. Herbalife was running north of 80%.

Ackman showed another slide showing Herbalife's top-selling product, Formula 1, and describes it as "a $2 billion brand nobody's ever heard of."[13] He shows a picture of this Formula 1, an Herbalife shake, and compares it with others: Oreos, Charmin, Crest, Gerber, Palmolive, Betty Crocker, Listerine, and Clorox. Formula 1 is a shake, but unlike competitive products made by GNC, Unilever, and Abbot Labs, it's a powder. Formula 1 doesn't even offer a ready-to-drink shake.

Herbalife sells 10 to 20 times as much powder as the competition, but it does so without a store. This is at the heart of Ackman's argument. Herbalife, he contends, is a pyramid scheme. Herbalife isn't selling its products to consumers, it's selling its products to distributors, who sell it, or don't, to consumers. "When you do the math, you find out your average club, these are the ten we went to in Queens, loses $12,000 a year." He then shares a video from one of the distributors, "Where your money's made is not serving smoothies. Where your money's made is having hundreds, or tens, or thousands of distributors around the globe who are working."

Ackman then asks, "How is it possible that Herbalife sells six times more nutrition powder than Abbot Labs, Unilever, and GNC combined? Perhaps it is cheaper … ?"

Nope, it's 65% more expensive (per 200 calories of serving) than the next most expensive product. All right, you get the point. But this goes on for hours and hundreds of slides.[14] He gets into the science of products, the patents, the R&D, he's read the annual reports and the SEC filings. He clearly has done his homework. No stone is left unturned. No cutlet is left uncooked, as Winston Churchill once said.

His three-hour presentation, which included 334 slides, was the latest in his years-long war with Herbalife. In 2012, he went on CNBC and said:

> You've had millions of low-income people around the world who've gotten their hopes up that there's an opportunity for them to become millionaires or hundred-thousand-aires or some number like that, and they've been duped. We simply want the truth to come out. If distributors knew the probability of making $95,000 a year – which is the millionaire team, as they call it—was a fraction of 1 percent, no one would ever sign up for this. And we simply exposed that fact. The company has done their best to try to keep that from the general public.[15]

He later would tell Bloomberg "This is the highest conviction I've ever had about any investment I've ever made."[16] Years later, he was still waging his war. In an interview with CNN, he repeatedly called the company a pyramid scheme.[17]

In those moments, Bill Ackman put himself in an almost impossible position. How could he ever admit defeat after telling everybody who would listen that this was a pyramid scheme that would go to zero? If he missed the mark on this, who would ever give him money again?

In the three days following his presentation, the stock had fallen 35%. The sell-off provided an opportunity for one of his biggest competitors to step in.

On January 9, Dan Loeb, founder of the hedge fund Third Point LLC, filed with the SEC, announcing that he had acquired 8.9 million Herbalife shares, or 8.24% of the stock, which made him the company's second largest shareholder. Loeb wrote a letter to his investors saying that the majority of his stake was purchased "during the panicked selling that followed the short seller's dramatic claims."[18] In the five days since Loeb's filing, Herbalife's stock rose 20%. Then a week later, the *Wall Street Journal* reported that billionaire activist investor Carl Icahn took a stake in Herbalife, and a month later, disclosures showed he owned 12.98% of the company.

Carl Icahn and Dan Loeb against Bill Ackman – a face-off raging all because Ackman got on his soapbox. It's impossible to know for sure whether Loeb and Icahn actually thought Herbalife was a good business and its stock was undervalued. In fact, that part was sort of irrelevant. What mattered was that Bill Ackman, by publicly acknowledging that he would go to the end of the world with this thing, just put a big, fat bull's-eye on his back. Just the idea that Ackman could be squeezed was enough to send the stock higher. A short squeeze is when a stock that someone has borrowed through a short sale, is forced to cover as the price rises dramatically against them. This is one of the dangerous things about shorting a stock; technically the upside is unlimited.

Herbalife hit a low of $24.24 in a few days after Ackman's first presentation and hasn't been below there since. It has gained 5% in a day 50 different times since 2012, and at $71.70, shares are currently 70% higher than where they were when he first shorted the stock.

The key to successful investing, especially when you're a contrarian, is to have people agree with you later. But when you're so public about your investments, whether you're running a hedge fund or your own brokerage account, it makes it so much harder. Dealing with your own emotions is challenging enough. Dealing with the emotions and pressure of others is even harder.

When we are verbal about our investments, we lose track of why we're investing in the first place, which is to make money. Outside pressures come in to play. Ackman didn't need the money. If his investors were the only ones who knew about his position, he could easily have said we're wrong, covered his position, and moved on. But apparently he would rather preserve his reputation than his investor's capital.

Having big public scores is incredibly profitable. Beyond just the gains you harvest for your existing client base, nothing attracts money in the hedge fund world like success. And nobody played up their successes better than Bill Ackman.

Bill Ackman once said, "If I think I'm right, I can be the most persistent and most relentless person in America."[19] During a presentation, Ackman shares a slide that said, "Why are pyramid schemes illegal? Pyramid schemes are said to be inherently fraudulent because they must eventually collapse."[20] Well maybe Herbalife is a pyramid scheme, and maybe it does eventually collapse, but will Ackman still be short if it does? Aside from the mental and emotional costs of watching a stock you short go against you, there is an actual financial cost to borrow the shares. You would think that at some point, regardless of how compelling the case against Herbalife is, his investors will scream uncle.

On July 25, 2016, the Federal Trade Commission charged Herbalife with four counts of unfair, false, and deceptive business practice. Herbalife paid $200 million to settle the complaint and said it would "fundamentally restructure its business." Herbalife's CEO described the settlement as "an acknowledgment that our business model is sound."[21] A year later, shares are up 11%.

During a Netflix documentary, *Betting On Zero*, Jon Silvan, a public relations strategist says, "Four hours later we get done with it, great presentation, and some genius in the audience looks at the stock and it's gone up. What's our response?" Ackman says, "It's irrelevant. It's not going up though." He argues this point, refusing to acknowledge that his short strategy was failing.[22] The stock was up 25% that day. Three years later, he's still short.

Notes

1. Fidelity Investments, "Fidelity Research Reveals Traders' Motivations beyond Investment Gains," press release, January 27, 2012.
2. E. S. Browning, "Fun Fades at Investing Clubs," *Wall Street Journal*, February 3, 2013.
3. Gretchen Morgenson and Geraldine Fabrikant, "A Rescue Ploy Now Haunts a Hedge Fund That Had It All," *New York Times*, January 19, 2003.
4. William D. Cohan, "The Big Short War," *Vanity Fair*, April 2013.
5. Jonathan R. Laing, "Meet Mr. Pressure," *Barron's*, December 5, 2005.
6. Ibid.
7. David Stowell, *Investment Banks, Hedge Funds, and Private Equity* (London: Academic Press, 2018), viii–x.
8. Jesse Eisinger, "Hedge-Fund Man at McDonald's," *Wall Street Journal*, September 28, 2005.
9. Bethany McLean, "Taking on McDonald's," *CNN Money*, December 15, 2005.
10. Joe Nocera, "Short Seller Sinks Teeth into Insurer," *New York Times*, December 1, 2007.
11. William D. Cohan, "Is Bill Ackman Toast?" *Vanity Fair*, October 17, 2016.
12. Cohan, "The Big Short War."
13. Steve Schaefer, "Ackman Takes Ax to Herbalife, Company 'Not an Illegal Pyramid Scheme,'" *Forbes*, December 20, 2012.
14. Pershing Square Capital Management, LP, "Who Wants to Be a Millionaire?" (presentation, December 20, 2012).
15. Bill Ackman, Interview with Andrew Ross Sorkin, *First on CNBC* breaking news interview, December 20, 2012.

16. Quoted in Cohan, "The Big Short War."
17. Bill Ackman, Interview with Cristina Alesci, *CNN Money*, July 22, 2014.
18. Cohan, "Is Bill Ackman Toast?"
19. Quoted in Nocera, "Short Seller."
20. Pershing Square Capital Management, "Who Wants to Be a Millionaire?"
21. Roger Parloff, "Herbalife Deal Poses Challenges for the Industry," *Fortune*, July 19, 2016.
22. *Betting on Zero* (motion picture), Filmbuff and Biltmore Films, 2016.

CHAPTER 10

Stanley Druckenmiller

Hard Lessons Can Be Necessary

> In a winner's game the outcome is determined by the correct actions of the *winner*. In a loser's game, the outcome is determined by mistakes made by the *loser*.[1]
>
> —Charlie Ellis

Charlie Ellis wrote this in his 1998 classic, *Winning the Loser's Game*. In other words, professionals *win* points and amateurs *lose* points. "Professional tennis players stroke the ball hard, with laserlike precision, through long and often exciting rallies until one player is able to drive the ball just out of reach or force the other player to make an error."[2] He contrasts this with how amateur games unfold. Instead of highly skilled shots and long volleys, amateur matches are full of faults, missed shots, and mistakes. It doesn't take much to draw the parallels between the way amateurs and professionals play tennis to the way amateurs and professionals play the market.

Amateur investors, and I'm painting with a broad brush, buy after stocks advance and sell after they decline. Cullen Roche said, "The stock market is the only market where things go on sale and all the customers run out of the store...."[3] This type of behavior, the desire to run for cover after you've been burned causes investors not just to underperform the market, but even their own investments. The spread between investment returns and investor returns is known as the behavior gap, and it is a permanent feature in any markets where human beings transact. It exists because the collective behavior of millions can overwhelm our senses. Fear and greed do not respond well when they're under assault. The market is notorious for forcing unforced errors.

The behavior gap is pervasive because the amateur investor gets fooled by averages. They're bombarded with information and literature suggesting that they can or should expect average returns, and they mistake average return for expected return. We frequently hear "stocks typically return between eight and ten percent a year." Well, over multiple decades, you could say they'll compound at between 8 and 10%, but the last time the Dow returned between 8 and 10% was 1952. There is a lot of space between what you expect the market to do and what it actually does, and this is where unforced errors lurk.

Stocks tend to swing in a wide range, spending a lot of time at the fringe and little time near the average, delivering maximum frustration. This sort of erratic behavior transfers money from the amateur's pocket and into the professional's.

US stocks have gained 30% or more 13 times annually. When this happens, the temptation is to look around at your friends and family to see how you stack up against other people. Bad things tend to happen when we compare our portfolios with others, especially if they possess a lesser IQ and extracted a higher return. On the flip side, and just as dangerous, there have been seven years where US stocks fell at least 30%. Big down years are massively disruptive to investor's long-term wealth, because people tend to run away from risk after it takes a bite out of their portfolio, which is like buying home insurance after a hurricane blows the roof off your house.

The amateur investor is most likely to make unforced errors at market tops and bottoms because, at the point of maximum optimism or pessimism, the story will have permeated throughout every corner of popular culture. When stocks are crashing *and* reverse crashing, the story will seem so compelling, that *not* making a change almost seems irresponsible.

Great investors do things differently than the rest of us. They buy what others don't want and sell what others crave. They're intimately familiar with the similarities between buying stocks and betting on the ponies. Michael Mauboussin says, "Fundamentals are how fast the horse runs and expectations are the odds."[4] This is what Howard Marks refers to as second-level thinking, and it escapes most of us. The casual investor thinks a good company makes for a good stock, without giving consideration to the fact that the majority of investors share a similar opinion. Perhaps, like-minded investors have pushed the price of a good company into that of a great company, making it less than it appears at first blush.

At a conference in 2015, the audience was introduced to one of the most successful investors of all time. In the introduction, he was compared to Warren Buffett, underscoring the speaker's tremendous success:

> Probably the poster child of investors, Warren Buffett in the last thirty years has compounded at just under 20%; $1,000 30 years ago would be $177,000 today, 24 up years and 6 down years ... 3 of the 6 were [down] more than 20%. Our speaker tonight, $1,000 invested with him 30 years ago, today it would be $2.6 million ... Thirty years, no losses.[5]

Stanley Druckenmiller is famous for taking the reins from George Soros and running his Quantum Fund for over a decade. He is one of the best global macro investors of all time. This game involves measuring economic sea changes and figuring out how they'll move stocks, bonds, and currencies around the globe. A colleague said, "Druckenmiller understood the stock market better than economists and understood economics better than stock pickers."[6] This was a unique combination. Add to this his affinity for risk management, and you've got a cocktail strong enough to knock his opponents on their behind. For three decades, he played the winner's game: "It's my philosophy, which has been reinforced by Mr. Soros, that when you earn the right to be aggressive, you should be aggressive. The years that you start off with a large gain are the times that you should go for it."[7]

Druckenmiller reportedly earned 30% a year for 30 years by throwing conventional wisdom in the trash can:

> The first thing I heard when I got in the business, not from my mentor, was bulls make money, bears make money, and pigs get slaughtered. I'm here to tell you I was a pig. And I strongly believe the only way to make long-term returns in our business that are superior is by being a pig.[8]

The most important lesson we can learn from one of the best to ever do it, one who earned billions by being a pig, is that even winners sometimes play the loser's game.

Druckenmiller dropped out of business school after just one semester and began his career at Pittsburgh National Bank. At 23 years old, he was by far the youngest in a group of eight other people. And then in 1978, not even two years after being hired, he was promoted to director of equity research. It wasn't apparent at the time that he would go on to become one of the best money managers ever. Instead, it was his youth, his clean slate that his boss found so appealing. He asked why he leapfrogged his peers, who had much more experience than he did. "For the same reason they send 18-year-olds to war. You're too dumb, too young, and too inexperienced not to know to charge. We around here have been in a bear market since 1968. I think a big secular bull market's coming. We've all got scars. We're not going to be able to pull the trigger. So I need a young, inexperienced guy to go in there and lead the charge." And lead the charge he did: Here's where my inexperience really paid off. When the Shah was deposed, I decided that we should put 70 percent of our money in oil stocks and the rest in defense stocks. . . . At the time, I didn't yet understand diversification."[9]

A few years later, Druckenmiller gave a presentation at a conference, and somebody in the audience came up to him after he was finished and said, "You're at a bank! What the hell are you doing at a bank? I'll pay you ten thousand dollars a month just to speak to you."[10]

With that, in February 1981, just 28 years old, Druckenmiller left the bank and launched Duquesne Capital Management. He started with $1 million under management and caught the upswing in small cap stocks in 1981. In just the first five months of the year, the Russell 2000 gained 14.92% while the S&P 500 fell 0.23%. He turned very bearish after the sharp advance, but he still managed to lose 12% in the third quarter, even though half of his portfolio was in cash. That led him to change his strategy. Druckenmiller was evolving. He was playing a winner's game.

Druckenmiller has one of the most interesting investing stories I've ever come across. In the first half of 1987, he was bullish while stocks were going straight up. The Dow Jones Industrial Average made 33 new highs in just the first four months of that year. It was up 45% at its highs in August, and after such a steep advance, Druckenmiller turned bearish in the summer. Sure enough, the market pulled back 17% from its August highs, and thinking there would be support at 2,200, he went from net short to 130% net long on October 16.[11] If you're familiar with "Black Monday," you already know 2,200 did not act as support.

The Dow closed at 2,246 on Friday and 1,738 on Monday. The 22.6% crash remains the single worst day ever for the US stock market. Stocks plunged at the open and subsequently bounced, and by lunchtime, Druckenmiller sold everything and went short! He covered his positions, and after a strong two-day bounce following Black Monday, Druckenmiller was again short the market. When stocks cratered on Thursday morning, he had made 25% in less than 24 hours. Druckenmiller was 130% net long going into the worst day in the history of the US stock market, and still made money in October 1987. He played the game at a level few ever have.

Druckenmiller was so talented that Dreyfus hired him in 1987 and let him continue running Duquesne. He ran the Strategic Aggressive Investing Fund, which was the best-performing fund in the industry from its inception (March 1987) until he left in 1988. He was soon managing seven different funds for Dreyfus[12] and quit to pursue his dream job, working for George Soros.

Druckenmiller was on the way to greatness on his own, but partnering with an iconic investor would eventually give him legendary status. In 1989, soon after his arrival, he shorted the Japanese stock market in a trade he described as "just about the best risk/reward trade I had ever seen."[13] Nearly 30 years later, with the Nikkei still 50% below its 1989 peak, this turned out to be a prescient call.

In August 1992, Druckenmiller was looking to short the British pound. At the time, Quantum had $7 billion in assets under management and, inspired by his mentor Soros, Druckenmiller looked at selling $5.5 billion in pounds and putting the money in Deutsche marks. It seemed risky to have almost the entire fund invested in a single trade, but Druckenmiller had worked the numbers and was confident it was a winner. Before taking action, he decided to run his idea past Soros. As he described his plan, Soros got a pained expression on his face. Just as Druckenmiller started to second guess his plan, Soros surprised him by saying, "That is the most ridiculous use of money management I have ever heard. What you described is an incredible one-way bet. We should have 200 percent of our net worth in this trade, not 100 percent."[14]

Druckenmiller and Soros put the equivalent of $2 for every $1 they had invested in the fund, and shorted the pound. The Bank of England spent $27 billion in an effort to defend their currency,[15] but it could not stand up to the onslaught of selling out of the Quantum Fund and others. When the levee broke and the pound crashed, Druckenmiller and Soros made a billion dollars.

Druckenmiller returned 31.5% in 1989, followed by 29.6%, 53.4%, 68.8%, and 63.2% in the next four years.[16] He put together one of the most remarkable investment records of all time, with huge sums of money, but not everything he touched turned to gold. Sooner or later, everybody hits the ball into the net.

Every macro investor will experience being flat-out wrong at some point in their career. In 1994, Druckenmiller had an $8 billion bet against the yen, nearly as large as his bet against the pound two years earlier. But when it rose 7% against the dollar, he lost $650 million in just two days.[17] Macro traders were wrecked; Paul Tudor Jones, Bruce Kovner, and Louis Bacon also got caught in the crossfire. Goldman Sachs had its worst year in a decade.[18] The Quantum Fund returned just 4% in 1994. This was better than the Dow, which gained 2%, or the S&P 500, which fell 1.5%, but the 4% return was much less than he and his investors were accustomed to.

In 1998, Quantum lost $2 billion in Russia. But this did not define his career or even his year. They still gained 12.4% for the year[19] and sidestepped the calamity that carried out Long-Term Capital Management feet first.

But just a year later, Druckenmiller *would* be carried out, and it wasn't because he misunderstood what a central bank was doing, or what the bond market was telling him. This time he committed the type of unforced error that is prevalent among amateur investors. He didn't just hit the ball into the net; he hit it onto another court.

In 1999, Druckenmiller made a $200 million bet against "overvalued" Internet stocks. In just a few weeks, the expensive stocks that he was betting would come back down to earth got more expensive. These early bets cost the fund $600 million and by May, he was down 18% for the year. Druckenmiller was out of touch with the market and that same month, he hired a young trader, not dissimilar to what his boss had done 20 years earlier. He attended the annual media and technology conference in Sun Valley, Idaho, where anyone who was anyone attended. Having drunk the Kool-Aid, when he came back to work, he gave his new hire more capital and brought in a second trader who was equally committed to the new investing paradigm. They were invested "in all this radioactive [stuff] that I don't know how to spell."[20] They righted the ship and finished the year up 35%.

An investor who made his living for 20 years by judging liquidity and which way the economic winds were blowing had no business investing in technology that he didn't understand. He knew this and quickly grew uncomfortable with his positions, so he took his gains and went back to where his bread was buttered, global macro. He was bullish on the newly created currency, the euro, but it went the opposite direction he thought it would. To add insult to injury, he watched in agony as the tech stocks he sold continued to soar while his two new employees were making money hand over fist. Druckenmiller's pride got in the way of his fear of the tech bubble. He didn't want to be upstaged by these young new traders, so he plowed his money back into tech.

Prior to the bubble bursting, Druckenmiller told the *Wall Street Journal*, "I don't like this market. I think we should probably lighten up. I don't want to go out like Steinhardt." But he didn't lighten up, and in fact, he backed up the truck. He bought VeriSign at $50, and at $240 a share, he doubled his bet to $600 million. As the tech sector began to wobble, VeriSign dropped to $135 and Soros wanted to reduce Quantum's holdings, but Druckenmiller wanted to stick it out. He was convinced VeriSign would remain steady and stand apart from the bubble.[21]

The NASDAQ peaked on March 10 and by April 14, just 25 days later, it had crashed 34%. VeriSign was no different from the rest of the floundering tech stocks. When the bubble burst, it was worth just 1.5% of what it was at its strongest point. "It would have been nice to go out on top, like Michael Jordan," Druckenmiller said at a news conference in late April. "But I overplayed my hand."[22] The Quantum Fund was down 21% for the year, and assets at Soros Fund Management fell by $7.6 billion since their peak in August 1998, of $22 billion.

Despite being the owner of one of the most impressive long-term track records, Druckenmiller remains humble and lighthearted. At the 2017 Ira Sohn conference he said, "Last year, I thought you should get out of equities and buy gold. That's why I'm introducing today and not presenting."[23]

There is a big difference between a lousy investment and an unforced error. Your thesis was wrong, or what you thought was already in the price; things like this are all part of the game. But oftentimes, we'll act impulsively, even when we "know" what we're doing is a mistake. Few people are spared from unforced errors, and the way they usually manifest themselves is because we can't handle people making money while we aren't. Munger once said:

> The idea of caring that someone is making money faster [than you] is one of the deadly sins. Envy is a really stupid sin because it's the only one you could never possibly have any fun at. There's a lot of pain and no fun. Why would you want to get on that trolley?[24]

Druckenmiller got on that trolley. He couldn't bear to see Quantum grinding its gears as a bunch of small-potato upstarts were racking up huge returns. Firms that were heavily into tech stocks were up as much as 50% for the year, while Quantum was stuck in single digits.

Druckenmiller knew exactly what he was doing – he just couldn't stop himself. "I bought $6 billion worth of tech stocks, and in six weeks I had lost $3 billion in that one play. You asked me what I learned. I didn't learn anything. I already knew that I wasn't supposed to do that. I was just an emotional basketcase and couldn't help myself. So maybe I learned not to do it again, but I already knew that."[25]

Maybe we all need to have this happen once or twice. Some things can't be taught, they have to be learned the hard way, even if we don't learn anything at all.

Notes

1. Charles D. Ellis, *Winning the Loser's Game*, 7th edition (New York: McGraw-Hill, 2017), 3–4.
2. Ibid.
3. Cullen Roche, posted on Twitter, @cullenroche, August 24, 2015.
4. Quoted in Michael Batnick. "When Something Is Obvious," *The Irrelevant Investor*, July 21, 2017.
5. Introduction to Stanley Druckenmiller's speech at the Lost Tree Club, Palm Beach, Florida, January 18, 2015.
6. Quoted in Sebastian Mallaby, *More Money Than God* (New York: Council on Foreign Relations, 2011), 148.
7. Jack D. Schwager, *The New Market Wizards* (New York: HarperBusiness, 1994, 197.
8. Druckenmiller, speech at the Lost Tree Club.
9. Ibid.
10. Schwager, *New Market Wizards*, 193.
11. Ibid., 230.
12. Ibid., 218.
13. Ibid., 237.
14. Mallaby, *More Money Than God*, 166.
15. Ibid.
16. Ibid., 150.
17. Ibid., 178.
18. Ibid., 180.
19. Edward Wyatt, "Market Place; Soros Advisers to Establish Separate Firm," *New York Times*, May 18, 1999.
20. Mallaby, *More Money Than God*, 258.
21. Quoted in Gregory Zuckerman, "How the Soros Funds Lost Game of Chicken against Tech Stocks," *Wall Street Journal*, May 22, 2000.
22. Quoted in Floyd Norris, "Another Technology Victim; Top Soros Fund Manager Says He 'Overplayed,'" *New York Times*, April 29, 2000.
23. Stanley Druckenmiller, introductory remarks, Ira Sohn Conference, New York, May 8, 2017.
24. Charlie Munger, opening comments, Wesco Annual Meeting, Pasadena, CA, May 7, 2003.
25. Druckenmiller, speech at the Lost Tree Club.

CHAPTER 11

Sequoia

The Risks of Concentrated Investing

> Your six best ideas in life will do better than all your other ones.
>
> —Bill Ruane

"Tis the part of a wise man to keep himself today for tomorrow, and not venture all his eggs in one basket." This timeless wisdom comes from Miguel de Cervantes's *Don Quixote,* which was published more than 400 years ago. Spreading your bets around is smart risk management and plain old common sense. A basket of 100 stocks exposes you to less idiosyncratic risk than a basket of just 10 stocks. If you hold 100 stocks, equally weighted, and one goes to zero, all else equal, you will have lost 1%. If you hold 10 stocks, equally weighted, and one goes to zero, all else equal, you will have suffered a 10% decline.

With a diversified US stock portfolio, one could have historically earned 8% a year. At that rate, it would take nine years to double your money. Certainly not bad, if you're starting with a large capital base, but nobody is going to retire at 40 by earning 8% annually. At that rate, it would take 91 years to turn $1,000 into $1 million. Diversification is one of the most basic principles in finance and lies at the center of modern portfolio theory. But why would you invest the same amount in your 20th best idea as your *very* best idea?

There's an old adage in finance, "Concentrate to get rich, diversify to stay rich." If you find one of the super compounders and hang on tight, you can build enormous fortunes in the stock market. When Warren Buffett first took control of Berkshire Hathaway stock in 1962, its market capitalization was around $22 million.[1] Berkshire gained 50% or more in a year 10 times and compounded at nearly 21% for 53 years, resulting in a $450 billion market capitalization today. Buffett did not become one of the richest men in the world by spreading his bets across his top 100 ideas.

Berkshire is in that rare group of stocks that is responsible for the majority of the market's long-term gains. The distribution of total stock market returns is heavily skewed toward these giant winners. The top 1,000 stocks alone, or less than 4% of the total public companies since 1926, have accounted for *all* of the market's gains. Exxon Mobil, Apple, Microsoft, General Electric, and IBM have each generated over half a trillion dollars in shareholder wealth.[2] The hunt for these potentially life-changing stocks motivates millions of market participants each day. But for every Berkshire Hathaway, there is a Sears Holdings, a GoPro for every IBM. While "concentrate to get rich" is certainly true, it's not wise financial advice. The stocks that produce these gigantic returns always appear obvious in hindsight, but in real time, finding and *holding* them is harder than hitting a 100 mph fastball. Concentrate in any one of the super compounders and you're a legend, but concentrate in a few losers and you're out of business.[3] Armed with this information, diversification sounds like a smart alternative.

Casual investors typically don't hold concentrated portfolios. Not many people working a 9 to 5 job have the time to dedicate to researching and monitoring this type of portfolio. But if you are one of those people, assuming you've done the necessary work that is required to have confidence in holding a big position, there are a plethora of risks to be aware of. First and most obvious, you might just be flat-out wrong. But this is merely the tip of the potential iceberg when it comes to things that can go wrong.

If you put in tens or maybe even hundreds of hours into researching a company, the sunk cost is very real, and potentially very expensive. The more time you've spent coming to a conclusion, the harder it is to change your mind. It's one thing for traders to buy and sell stocks at a machine-gun pace. You buy this stock and it's not working, so get rid of it. But for the fundamental investor, if what you consider to be one of your top ideas isn't working, you're more likely to add to the position than you are to come to the conclusion that you missed something. If you loved the stock at $100, at $90 you're buying more, and at $80 you're thanking the market gods for this opportunity. But what do you do at $70, $60, and $50? This isn't just theoretical, this should be expected. Almost all of the best stocks get killed, however, they don't all come back, and it's only with the benefit of hindsight that we can separate the winners from the losers.

Investors can learn of the dangers embedded in running a concentrated portfolio by studying one of the most successful mutual funds of all time, one that was able to separate the winners from the losers, went all in on their best ideas, and beat the market for decades – the Sequoia Fund.

Sequoia is run by Ruane, Cunniff & Goldfarb, which, since 1970, has been utilizing a long-term strategy based on extensive research honed to outperform the S&P 500 Index. According to *The Washington Post*, "It's not unheard of for a Sequoia analyst to spend a decade investigating a company, going to annual meetings, talking to dozens of employees, managers, customers, suppliers."[4] Can you imagine spending a decade researching a company that you don't even own? What if while you're watching it, the stock gains 500%? How do you not kick yourself for buying earlier?

And how is it possible to spend 10 years studying the company and then *not buy?*

Sequoia is not interested in short-term profits, or 1% positions. They expect to hold their stocks for a long period of time and to earn a significant return above and beyond an index. To achieve long-term success with this type of approach requires exhaustive due diligence. One of Sequoia's holdings, O'Reilly Automotive, an auto parts retailer, was one such success story. In 2004, when Sequoia bought, O'Reilly was worth $19.84. By year end 2017, it was worth about $240, despite suffering a nearly 40% drawdown that year. But winning that big takes a lot of planning. Fund director, John B. Harris, did extensive research on O'Reilly, which included visiting 100 stores.[5] The fund and its investors aren't shedding any tears over the recent drawdown as it was the rare 10-bagger that eludes most investors. But Sequoia's intensive research doesn't always result in a happy ending, and the fund was front and center in one of the biggest disasters in the history of concentrated positions.

The website of Ruane, Cunniff & Goldfarb, Sequoia's firm, describes their strategy like this:

> In managing the Fund, Ruane, Cunniff pursues a value-oriented approach, seeking to outperform over the long-term by purchasing shares, at prices below our estimated range of their intrinsic values, in high-quality businesses that have significant and durable competitive advantages.[6]

If that sounds exactly like something Warren Buffett would write, it's not a coincidence, Sequoia's story cannot be written without him. Not only was Berkshire Hathaway its largest holding from 1990 to 2010, but also Buffett is the reason Sequoia exists in the first place.

In 1969, Warren Buffett decided to close his limited partnership. He had felt, rightly, that the market had gotten so far ahead of itself, in terms of price relative to value, that there weren't enough opportunities to invest with the margin of safety that he sought. But he did not want to leave his investors to navigate the coming turbulent waters on their own, because he knew a shark would come along and drag them under. So he hand-selected Bill Ruane to be the steward of their capital. As he wrote in his famous essay, "The Superinvestors of Graham-and-Doddsville":

> When I wound up Buffett Partnership I asked Bill if he would set up a fund to handle all of our partners so he set up the Sequoia Fund.

He set it up at a terrible time, just when I was quitting. He went right into the two-tier market and all the difficulties that made for comparative performance for value oriented investors.[7]

Not surprisingly to Buffett, stocks did poorly over the next few years and value stocks did even worse. Sequoia got off to a rough start, underperforming the S&P 500 in each of its first three years. Since its inception in the middle of 1970 through the end of 1973, $1 shrank to $0.85. Things were so bad that Bill Ruane and Richard Cunniff almost shut it down in 1974.[8] But they didn't, and with the help of Buffett's loyal acolytes, they persevered.

The early investors that stuck with the fund have been handsomely rewarded. Sequoia has outperformed the S&P 500 by 2.6% a year for 47 years.[9] $10,000 invested in July 1970 would have grown to nearly $4 million today. This is three times as much as one could have earned by buying and holding the S&P 500.[10]

Every investment strategy that doesn't deviate from its core tenets, whether its value or trend following or anything else, will have long periods of time where it looks and feels foolish. The dot-com bubble was that period for all value investors, including Ruane & Cunniff. In 1999 the Sequoia Fund lost 16.5% while the S&P 500 gained 21% and the tech-heavy NASDAQ Composite gained 86%! At the time, Sequoia was running a super concentrated portfolio of just 12 stocks, with 37% invested in Berkshire Hathaway. When the tide turned and value got its vogue back, investors who stayed with Sequoia were vindicated. From 2000 through 2002, the fund gained 29% as the S&P 500 (total return) fell 38%.[11] Sequoia has experienced tough times and bounced back, but it remains to be seen whether or not they come back from their most recent saga. It's understandable when value investors don't keep up in a market driven by growth stocks, but Sequoia's recent setback has nothing to do with the current market regime. This wound was self-inflicted.

In Sequoia's 2010 annual report, they told investors that they were evolving, that the super-concentrated portfolios were a thing of the past. "Another gradual change at Sequoia has been an increase in the number of holdings. At the end of 2010, we held 34 stocks in the Fund, which we believe is an all-time high."[12] But you can't teach an old investor new tricks, and the Sequoia Fund would be back to its concentrated ways in short order.

It was in that same report, ironically, that they introduced what would become an extraordinarily large position, Valeant Pharmaceuticals. They first began purchasing shares on April 28, 2010, at $16. Valeant gained 70% that year and it quickly became the fund's second largest holding. Through the first three months of 2011, Valeant gained another 76%, and for the first time in 20 years, Berkshire Hathaway was no longer their largest holding. That year, with Valeant's wind at their backs, they outperformed the S&P 500 by double digits for the first time since 2003.[13]

The fund was doing great and investor demand was so strong that assets under management had nearly tripled from the time they first bought Valeant. The fund did what few responsible stewards of capital do – they shut it to new investors. (This was not the first time this happened. Sequoia closed to new investors from 1982 until 2008.)[14]

They rode Buffett's coattails and they planned to do the same of Valeant CEO, Mike Pearson, whom they described as "exceptionally capable and shareholder focused ... We think he is ideally suited to run a business that is at heart a value investor in pharmaceutical products."[15]

Sequoia described Valeant as "A pharmaceutical company that doesn't spend much money on research and development.... While Valeant doesn't spend much money on R&D, it does invest heavily in its sales force."[16] Valeant didn't spend much money on R&D because its business model relied not on creating new drugs, but buying existing ones and then raising the prices. For example, in 2013, Valeant bought Medicis, whose calcium disodium versenate drug was used to treat people exposed to lead poisoning. The original cost was $950, which Valeant raised to $27,000.[17] Mike Pearson was certainly shareholder focused, but that is where he and Warren Buffett's similarities ended. Talking about Pearson, Buffett said, "If you're looking for a manager you want someone who is intelligent, energetic, and moral. But if they don't have the last one, you don't want them to have the first two."[18]

In September 2015, presidential candidate Hillary Clinton tweeted, "Price gouging like this in the specialty drug market is outrageous. Tomorrow I'll lay out a plan to take it." In that session and the five to follow, Valeant shares fell 31%. Valeant was being punished for what many considered to be unethical business practices, but raising drug prices is hardly a rarity in the healthcare industry. What would really knock Valeant off its perch were accusations of fraud.

On October 21, 2015, Citron Research published a report, accusing Valeant of accounting fraud and compared it to Enron.[19] That day, shares collapsed nearly 40% before recovering and closing "only" down 19%. As a result of its huge position, that month Sequoia underperformed the S&P 500 by 17.47%! (The fund lost 9.03% as the S&P 500 gained 8.44%.)

With Valeant shares down more than 50% from their highs and fraudulent accusations ripping across Wall Street, Sequoia put out a letter to its shareholders. "Its chief executive, J. Michael Pearson, has in our opinion done a masterful job of acquiring a broad portfolio of prescription drugs."[20] Of Pearson they said, "He has been aggressive every step of the way, and has attracted equally aggressive critics."

Sequoia didn't just say this to calm their investors, they actually believed it. So they did what value investors do when their stock gets crushed – they bought more. After this purchase, Sequoia became Valeant's single largest shareholder, and it represented 32% of the fund's assets. During the panic, invoking an old Buffett line, David Poppe, CEO of Ruane, Cunniff said, "Be greedy when others are fearful." He also used Berkshire to defend his choice, saying that when Berkshire got crushed in the late nineties, it was 35% of the fund while the stock got cut in half. True, Berkshire recovered and was one of their best investments ever,[21] but while the comparison might have made him feel better about buying another 1.5 million shares of Valeant, it did nothing to calm their investors.

Michael Pearson is no Warren Buffett and Valeant is no Berkshire Hathaway. Thomas Heath from *The Washington Post* described it like this: "What Sequoia married itself to was an offshore drug company that borrowed heavily to buy other drug companies, cut costs and research, then raised prices on many older drugs to astronomical heights."[22]

Eight months after defending Pearson and Valeant, Sequoia would sell their entire position. Valeant lost more than 90% of its value in just a few months, and Sequoia, which had hitched its wagon to Valeant, saw its assets cut in half.[23] An investor base that expected results had long replaced the patient investors that they began with in 1970. Losing 26.7% in a 12-month period when the S&P 500 gained 4% was too much to bear. In 2013, Sequoia closed the fund to keep new investors out; as a result of the Valeant crisis, it could have used a lock to keep them in. In just a few months, Sequoia assets fell from more than $9 billion to under $5 billion. A single stock leveled one of the most successful funds of all time, you should think twice before putting yourself in the same type of situation.

If you want to make big money in the stock market, you have two choices: (1) buy a lot of stocks, an index fund, for example, and hold them for a long time (even then, no guarantees) or (2) buy a few stocks and hope you're right. Sequoia was right for a long time, and then they were very wrong. Even with the Valeant debacle, their long-term track record is phenomenal, but the point in all this is that if you are going to take concentrated positions, you must have the stomach for massively different results than the overall market. It's easy to look at long-term charts of Microsoft and Apple in awe, but when you do, remind yourself of Valeant and Enron.

There are a few things you can do to prevent yourself from marrying the next Valeant. If you are buying a chipmaker because you hope it gets into the next iPhone, write down your thinking. This way, if it doesn't come to fruition, you can combat the endowment effect, which is the phenomenon of people ascribing more value to something because they own it. Writing down the reason you bought something can mitigate this. The other thing you can do to prevent your own future self from getting stuck to a position is to write down an exit plan. For example, Let's say I am putting 10% of my portfolio in stock XYZ at $100, and I'm willing to risk 5% of my overall portfolio on this stock. Then you can back into the price at which you would cut your losses, in this case, all else equal, if stock XYZ falls below $50, you're out.

Diversification is slow and boring, concentration is fun and exciting. But if fun and exciting is what you seek, the stock market can be a very expensive place to find it.

Notes

1. Warren Buffett, 1994 Berkshire Hathaway annual letter, March 7, 1995.
2. Hendrick Bessembinder, "Do Stocks Outperform Treasury Bills?," *Journal of Financial Economics*, November 22, 2017.
3. Ibid.
4. Thomas Heath, "An Epic Winning Streak on Wall Street – Then One Ugly Loss," *Washington Post*, August 12, 2017.
5. Ibid.
6. Ruane, Cunniff & Goldfarb, "Sequoia Fund," www.sequoiafund.com, December 2017.
7. Warren Buffett, "The Superinvestors of Graham-and-Doddsville," *Hermes* (New York: Columbia Business School, 1984).
8. Ruane, Cunniff & Goldfarb, 2016 Sequoia Fund annual report, December 31, 2016.

9. Author's calculation.
10. Author's calculation. Note that the first S&P 500 index fund was not created until 1976, so such an investment would have been impossible until that year.
11. Author's calculations using data from Bloomberg.
12. Ruane, Cunniff & Goldfarb, 2010 Sequoia Fund annual report, December 31, 2010.
13. Ibid.
14. Steven Goldberg, "What I Learned from Sequoia Fund's Tragic Love Affair with Valeant," *Kiplinger*, April 29, 2016.
15. Ibid.
16. Ibid.
17. StreetInsider.com, "Imprimis Pharma (IMMY) Announces Lower-Cost Option to Valeant's (VRX) Lead Poisoning Treatment," October 17, 2016.
18. Quoted in Bob Bryan, "Warren Buffett and Charlie Munger Just Destroyed Valeant at Berkshire's Annual Meeting," *Business Insider*, April 30, 2016.
19. Citron Research, "Valeant: Could This Be the Pharmaceutical Enron?," October 21, 2015.
20. Ruane, Cunniff & Goldfarb, Letter to Shareholders, October 28, 2015.
21. James B. Stewart, "Huge Valeant Stake Exposes Rift at Sequoia Fund," *New York Times*, November 12, 2015.
22. Heath, "An Epic Winning Streak."
23. Lucinda Shen, "Valeant's Second Largest Investor Just Dumped the Rest of Its Stock," *Fortune*, July 13, 2017.

CHAPTER 12

John Maynard Keynes

The Most Addictive Game

How could economics not be behavioral? If it isn't behavioral, what the hell is it?

—Charlie Munger

The cost of raising a child today is $233,610.[1] This is a 41% increase over the past 15 years, or 2.3% a year.[2]

From gasoline to food to education and raising children, prices tend to rise over time. Staying ahead of inflation is why millions of Americans invest. But what about the one-tenth of one percenters who have more money than they can spend in 4,000 lifetimes? Why do they still invest? I'm not talking about wealthy people who invest for future generations, but billionaires who spend the entirety of their sixth and seventh decades trying to beat the S&P 500.

A 60-year-old with a billion dollars can spend more than $90,000 a day until their 90th birthday. So if the purpose of investing is to defer current consumption for future benefit, there has to be another reason why these people spend so much time trying to beat the market when they've already won. The reason why some billionaires are still consumed by the market is because these people are driven to climb mountains, and putting all the market's pieces together is the Everest of intellectual challenges. In a 1987 documentary, *Trader,* Paul Tudor Jones says:

> During my second semester senior year in college he said I've always liked backgammon, chess, those type of games, and he said if you think those are fun, if you really enjoy that type of stimulation, then I'll show you a game that is the most exciting and most challenging of all.[3]

Jones continued to explain that once he reached a particular mark, he would stop and retire. He didn't specify what that number was, but it's now 30 years later, he's been a billionaire for a long time, and he's still running his fund.

Every minute of every day, markets are putting out clues, little crumbs of information for would-be market detectives. This is the most addictive game on the planet because it's a game that never ends. The pieces are always zigging and zagging and by the time you think you've got things figured out, new rules are implemented. Where are interest rates today and where are they going tomorrow? How has the economy performed over the past 12 months and what will the next 12 look like? How are markets behaving? And not just stocks, but what about currencies and commodities and real estate and bonds? This is the macro game, and it has destroyed many more fortunes than it's created.

Even if we had tomorrow's news today, we couldn't know how markets would react because the laws of physics do not govern them. There is no $E = MC^2$. If you drop an eight-sided ball, there's no way to predict which way it would bounce. The same idea holds true in finance – Serotonin plus adrenaline plus different time horizons times a few million participants equals *literally nobody knows*.

Let's pretend that we knew with complete certainty that Apple's earnings will grow by 8% a year for the next decade. Would this give you the confidence to buy its stock? It shouldn't, and here's why. How fast is the overall market growing and how fast are investors expecting Apple to grow? Even if we have clairvoyance on the most important driver of long-term returns, earnings, it wouldn't be enough to ensure success. The missing ingredient, which *cannot* be modeled by all the PhDs in the world, is investor's moods and expectations. Investing with perfect information is difficult – investing with imperfect information and cognitive biases has made mincemeat out of millions of investors.

When you're betting on sports or horses, you can't know who's going to win, but at least you know the odds. If you have a feeling that the Golden State Warriors are going to win the finals next year, you're not alone. The Warriors are the favorites to win the championship and the market, or the betting odds in this case, reflect the current optimism. If you bet $100 on the Warriors winning the finals in 2018 and they do, you'd receive only $60.61. On the other hand, if you bet on the New York Knicks, a long shot, a $100 wager would payout $50,000![4] Steven Crist, a famous handicapper, explains this idea perfectly, "Even a horse with a very high likelihood of winning can be either a very good or a very bad bet, and the difference between the two is determined by only one thing: the odds."[5]

The parallels between betting on the horses or the Warriors and betting on stocks or commodities are obvious, but there is one major difference: With investing, the odds are determined by investor's expectations, and they're *not* published on any website. They're not quantifiable because they're subject to our manic highs and depressive lows. You can have all the information in the world, but humans set prices, and decisions are rarely made with perfect information.

Few people understood the disconnect between what the market *should* do and what it actually does better than one of the most infamous names in all of finance, John Maynard Keynes. He once said that:

> Professional investment may be likened to those newspaper compe-titions in which the competitors have to pick out the six prettiest faces from a hundred photographs … each competitor has to pick, not those faces which he himself finds prettiest, but those which he thinks likeliest to catch the fancy of the other competitors … We have reached the third degree where we devote our intelligences to anticipating what average opinion expects the average opinion to be.[6]

Investors can learn a lot from Keynes, who learned that trying to beat the market by anticipating what average opinion expects the average opin-ion to be is a game that's not worth playing.

Chapter 12 of Keynes's *The General Theory of Employment, Interest and Money* is one of the most influential things ever written in finance. Jack Bogle wrote, "That chapter, laced with investment wisdom, made a major impact on my 1951 senior thesis … Keynes the *investor*, not the *economist*, has been the inspiration for my central investment philosophy."[7] Warren Buffett said, "If you understand chapters 8 and 20 of *The Intelligent Investor* and chapter 12 of *The General Theory*, you don't need to read anything else and you can turn off your TV."[8] George Soros wrote, "I fancied myself as some kind of god or an economic reformer like Keynes."[9] Finally, the intellectual giant Peter Bernstein credits Keynes with defining risk "as it has come to be understood today."[10] What was it about Keynes that made these financial giants speak with such reverence?

Keynes wrote several international best-selling books, revolutionized institutional asset management, and practically built the global monetary system as we know it. He designed England's financing of World War II, and he was hugely influential in designing the Bretton Woods agreement, which established the postwar global monetary system. When Keynes died, the obituary in *The Times* read, "To find an economist of comparable influ-ence, one would have to go back to Adam Smith."[11] Keynes was so far ahead of his time that when John Kenneth Galbraith reviewed his semi-nal work, *The General Theory of Employment, Interest and Money*, he wrote, "The economists of established reputation had not taken to Keynes. Faced with the choice of changing one's mind versus proving that there is no need to do so, almost everyone opts for the latter."[12]

Keynes received his education at King's College, Cambridge, and began his professional career in 1906 as a civil servant in the revenue, statistics and commerce department of England's India office. A few years later, he began lecturing at Cambridge University.

After World War I, the global monetary system was left in tatters. Keynes was the Treasury's representative at the peace conference in Versailles, but he vehemently disagreed with how the Allies wanted to be compensated for war damages. The reparations they were placing on Germany were far too punitive and would destroy the country's currency as well as their economy, and leave both sides in a lose-lose position. Keynes wouldn't go along with this, so he resigned, writing to Prime Minister David Lloyd George, "I ought to let you know that on Saturday I am slipping away from this scene of nightmare. I can do no more good here."[13]

Following his resignation, he spilled his thoughts into what quickly became an international best seller, *The Economic Consequences of the Peace*. In it he wrote, "Lenin was certainly right. There is no subtler, no surer means of overturning the existing basis of society than to debauch the currency." Prophetically, he wrote, "If we aim deliberately at the impoverishment of Central Europe, vengeance, I dare predict, will not be limp."[14]

With money pouring in from book royalties and speaking engagements, Keynes decided to leverage his knowledge of the economic machine by speculating in currencies. Prior to the war, currencies were fixed, but after they were left to float, giving opportunities to investors with superior insight. He felt that postwar inflation would hurt the French franc and especially the German Reichsmark, so he shorted those currencies and a few others. He earned $30,000 in just a few months—so he took the next logical step. He set up a syndicate in 1920 to manage money professionally for friends and family. This also got off to a good start, they made $80,000 by the end of April 1920.[15] But then, over just a four-week period, a brief wave of optimism spread across the continent, and the currencies he shorted quickly rose in value, wiping out all of syndicate's capital. When he was forced to close it, every single currency position was underwater.[16] Keynes was bailed out by his father, and not deterred by this blow up, he was able to rebound, kept speculating, and built up a capital base of $120,000 by the end of 1922, nearly $2 million in today's dollars.[17]

Keynes then got heavily into commodity speculation, applying the same top down approach that he did to currencies. Instead of investing in the extremely volatile franc and Reichsmark and rupee, he turned to tin and cotton and wheat. This endeavor ended in a similar way to the previous one. When the great crash came and commodities were decimated, Keynes lost 80% of his net worth.

In 1924, Keynes became First Bursar at King's College and took control of the college's finances. He was still finding his way as an investor and his evolution would take a few years. Anybody who has ever tried his or her hand in the market has had the feeling that Keynes did in the 1920s. We open up a newspaper and start constructing top-down views of how the world is functioning. But figuring out how interest rates affect currencies and how labor affects prices and how all of this affects our investments is tantamount to putting together a three dimensional puzzle where the pieces are always moving.

When Keynes assumed control over the endowment fund, it was severely constrained by what it could invest in. At that time, the world of institutional asset management focused heavily on real estate and bonds. Stocks were seen as too risky and were eschewed by most institutional managers. But he was able to convince them to separate a piece of it into a discretionary portfolio, which left him free to do whatever he wanted. Elroy Dimson, professor at Cambridge, studied the records and concluded that over the period 1922–1946, this portfolio had a 16% average annual return, compared with 10.4% for a market index.[18] (Keynes's investing style evolved over the years, and the methods that he employed during the first half of his tenure looked nothing like what he would ultimately use to achieve those outsized returns.)

When he took over the fund, he sold properties so that he could invest in the stock market. Keynes thought he would fare better speculating in an asset that had daily price quotes and liquidity than investing in something over which he had little control. But he was highly levered when the crash came, and the belief that his ability to track credit cycles and economic expansions and contractions had failed him. The fund lost in 32% in 1930 and another 24% in 1931.[19] He had misread the current conditions, and his macro insights after the crash were no better. "With low interest rates, enterprise throughout the world can get going again … commodity prices will recover and farmers will find themselves in better shape."[20]

Keynes had accomplished more in 10 years than most economists would accomplish in a lifetime, and brilliant as he was, his superior intellect did not provide him with superior insights into short-term market movements. In studying his commodities trading, it was difficult to get a clear record of *exactly* how he fared because his turnover was so high. He suffered like I did and so many other investors do, from the illusion of control. He thought that by trading so frequently, he could control his own destiny and achieve success. He was wrong. He took this style with him to the King's College endowment, and delivered negative alpha for the first few years.

It wasn't just the college that suffered at Keynes's hands; he was running an investment pool that was liquidated after the crash. "Although Keynes was well known for his arrogance and his air of intellectual superiority, the humbling experience of having nearly lost two fortunes changed his thinking on the best way to invest."[21] Keynes did a complete 180, shifting his thinking from being a short-term speculator to a long-term investor. The psychological forces of the market consumed him, and this made his obsession with the macro economy and the link between currencies and interest rates and stock prices seem completely irrelevant.

He began studying companies, looking at cash flows and earnings and dividends, with a sharp focus on businesses that were selling for less than their intrinsic value. Keynes went from macro to micro, top down to bottom up, and with this new vision, he was able to build a fortune for himself, King's College, and two insurance companies. Keynes put his ego to the side and gave up trying to forecast interest rates and currencies and how they affect the economy. As a long-term value investor, he bought "Securities where I am satisfied as to assets and to ultimate earning power and where the market price seems cheap in relation to these."[22] Keynes is the father of macroeconomics, but ironically, his investing success occurred once he was able to adopt something that was the antithesis of this.

If you can buy something for less than its intrinsic value, you give yourself a better chance over the long-term than trying to outguess your competition over the short-term. Keynes wrote about this in chapter 12 of *The General Theory*:

> If we speak frankly, we have to admit that our basis of knowledge for estimating the yield ten years hence of a railway, a copper mine, a textile factory, the goodwill of a patent medicine, an Atlantic liner, a building in the City of London amounts to little and sometimes to nothing; or even five years hence.[23]

His leap into value investing, successful as it was, presented its own set of challenges. Value, like anything else, is seasonal, and you'll never know ahead of time when summer will turn to winter. From 1936 to 1938, Keynes lost two-thirds of his wealth, and the portfolios he was managing didn't fare much better. The boards of two insurance companies whose money he was managing were livid with his performance. National Mutual lost £641,000,[24] and when they asked him to explain his performance, he wrote:

> I don't not believe that selling at very low prices is a remedy for having failed to sell at high ones.... I do not think it is the business, far less the duty, of an institutional or any other serious investor to be constantly considering whether he should cut and run on a falling market.... The idea that we should all be selling out to the other fellow and should all be finding ourselves with nothing but cash at the bottom of the market is not merely fantastic, but destructive of the whole system.[25]

This is a quantum leap from where his head was at just a decade earlier.

King's College also wanted answers, so two months later, in a memo to the Estates Committee of King's College, he wrote:

> The idea of wholesale shifts is for various reasons impracticable and indeed undesirable. Most of those who attempt it sell too late and buy too late, and do both too often.... I believe now that successful investment depends upon three principles:
>
> A careful selection of few investments having regard to their cheapness in relation to their probable actual and potential intrinsic value over a period of years ahead and in relation to alternative investments at the time.
>
> A steadfast holding of these in fairly large units through thick and thin, perhaps for several years, until they have fulfilled their promise or it is evident that they were purchased on a mistake;
>
> A balanced investment position, i/e, a variety of risks in spite of individual holdings being large, and if possible opposed risks.[26]

The intellectual flexibility for a macro economist, one with a huge ego no less, to shift from top-down to bottom-up is truly remarkable. He surrendered to the reality that forecasting investor's moods is nearly impossible and mostly a waste of time.

Everybody likes to think they're long-term investors, but we don't pay enough attention to the fact that life is lived in the short term. In *A Tract on Monetary Reform*, Keynes wrote, "This *long run* is a misleading guide to current affairs. *In the long run* we are all dead."[27] Long-term returns are all that matters to investors, but our portfolios are marked to market every day, so when short-term turbulence arrives, long-term thinking flies out the window. Keynes referred to our tendency to get swept up by short-term thinking as *animal spirits*, which he described as "a spontaneous urge to action rather than inaction, and not as the outcome of a weighted average of quantitative benefits multiplied by quantitative probabilities."[28] Keynes is one of the rare investors that was not only aware of his cognitive biases but was able to effectively combat them.

From 1928 to 1931, King's College's assets fell nearly 50%, compared to just a 30% decline for the UK stock market. But from 1932 to 1945, Keynes grew the fund by 869%. The UK market for comparison had grown by just 23% over the same time![29] The change from short-term speculation to long-term investing made all the difference. The portfolio turnover averaged 56% during the first half of this period and fell to only 14% in the second half.[30]

Before Thaler's *Nudge*, Shiller's *Irrational Exuberance*, and Kahneman and Tversky's Prospect Theory, there were Keynes's *animal spirits*. He realized that he could have all the information in the world, but without the ability to control his own behavior, and predict the behavior of others, it was less than meaningless.

Keynes was able to deliver remarkable investment results in a period that encompassed the crash of 1929 and the subsequent Great Depression, as well as World War II. He was able to achieve these results because he stopped trying to play the impossible game of outthinking everybody else in the near term. Figuring out what the average opinion expects the average opinion to be was beyond even one of the most brilliant men to ever lace 'em up. The lesson for us mortals is obvious: Do not play this game! Think long term and focus on asset allocation.

Successful investors construct portfolios that allow them to capture enough of the upside in a bull market without feeling as if they're getting left behind, and a portfolio that allows them to survive a bear market when everyone around them is losing their mind. This is no small feat, simple as this sounds; this is a very difficult exercise.

The most disciplined investors are intimately aware of how they'll behave in different market environments, so they hold a portfolio that is suited to their personality. They don't kill themselves trying to build a perfect portfolio because they know that it doesn't exist. Rather, they embrace what Keynes is incorrectly attributed to have said: "It is better to be roughly right than precisely wrong."

Notes

1. Kathryn Vasel, "It Costs $233,610 to Raise a Child," *CNN Money*, January 9, 2017.
2. Jessica Dickler, "The Rising Cost of Raising a Child," *CNN Money*, September 21, 2011.
3. *Trader*, Public Broadcasting Service (PBS), 1987.
4. Odds Shark, odds calculator.
5. Steven Crist, "Steven Crist on Value," ValueWalk, September 10, 2016.
6. John Maynard Keynes, *General Theory of Employment, Interest, and Money* (New York: Harvest/Harcourt, 1964), Chapter 12. (Originally published in 1935.)
7. John C. Bogle, "Keynes the Investor," foreword to *Way to Wealth* by John F. Wasik (New York: McGraw-Hill Education, 2013), x.
8. Quoted in John Wasik, "Warren Buffett's Secret Sauce," *Forbes*, February 26, 2014.
9. George Soros, *The Alchemy of Finance* (Hoboken, NJ: Wiley, 2003), 372. (Originally published in 1987.)
10. Peter L. Bernstein, *Against the Gods* (New York: Wiley, 1996), 217.
11. Louis M. Hacker, "John Maynard Keynes: He Casts a Long Shadow, but Was He Right?," *New York Times*, June 28, 1959.
12. John K. Galbraith, "'Came the Revolution,' Review of Keynes' *General Theory*," *New York Times Book Review*, May 16, 1965.
13. "John Maynard Keynes – Timeline," MaynardKeynes.org, December 2017.
14. John Maynard Keynes, *The Economic Consequences of the Peace* (New York: HarperCollins, 1971). (Originally published in 1919.)
15. Liaquat Ahamed, *Lords of Finance* (New York: Penguin, 2009), 165.
16. John F. Wasik, *Way to Wealth* (New York: McGraw-Hill Education, 2013), 19.
17. Ahamed, *Lords of Finance*, 165.
18. Nitin Mehta, "Keynes the Investor: Lessons to Be Learned," 2017 CFA Institute European Investment Conference, Berlin, Germany, November 16–17, 2017.

19. MaynardKeynes.org, "Keynes the Investor," December 2017.
20. Quoted in Polly Hill. *Lydia and Maynard* (New York: Scribner, 1990), 17.
21. Wasik, *Way to Wealth*, 48.
22. Letter to the chairman of the Provincial insurance company, 1942.
23. Keynes, *General Theory of Employment, Interest, and Money*, Chapter 12.
24. Wasik, *Way to Wealth*, 109.
25. Ibid.
26. John Maynard Keynes, "Memorandum for the Estates Committee, Kings College," Cambridge, UK, 1938.
27. John Maynard Keynes, *A Tract on Monetary Reform* (New York: Macmillan, 1924).
28. Keynes, *General Theory of Employment, Interest, and Money*, Chapter 12.
29. Author's calculations using data from MaynardKeynes.org, "Keynes the Investor."
30. Mehta, "Keynes the Investor."

CHAPTER 13

John Paulson

You Only Need to Win Once

Quit while you're ahead. All the best gamblers do.

—Baltasar Gracian

Ask somebody what they would wish for if a genie appeared before them and having a lot of money would be a top answer. But "be careful what you wish for" is a cliché for a very good reason.

William "Bud" Post III won $16.2 million in the Pennsylvania lottery in 1988 and upon his death in 2006, he was living off Social Security payments of about $450 per month.[1] Evelyn Adams also won the lottery. Twice. Despite winning a total of $5.4 million, 20 years later she was broke and living in a trailer.[2] These stories are not just anecdotal. They are far more common than you would think; nearly one-third of all lottery winners lose it all.[3] Winning the lottery is 100% luck. Successful investing on the other hand is a combination of good fortune and superior skill.

The stock market is the biggest casino in the world, and there is no shortage of ways to cash in. With options, levered ETFs, and futures contracts, there are thousands of different tables for investors to sit at. And the best thing about getting lucky in the market, aside from the obvious, is that your brokerage account doesn't put you on trial. "Did the stock double for reasons you thought it would? What was the basis of your decision!?!" Money earned by luck is indistinguishable from money earned by skill.

Investing is a fierce game of brains and desire. The people you're competing with have endless resources and unlimited access to information, so it's far more likely for you to get lucky than it is to consistently run faster than the competition.

While it's nice to make money by chance, the downside of getting lucky in the market is that we tend to attribute the success more to skill than we do to randomness. We then transfer this confidence into our next investment. If one-third of all lottery winners go bust, then three-thirds of lucky investors revert to the mean. On this very issue, Michael Mauboussin said: "The main issue is that putting yourself in a position to enjoy good luck also puts you in a position to lose."[4] Once you've achieved a great deal of success, failure is usually not far behind. When investors catch a lucky break, it's rare that people walk to the cashier, hand in their chips, and ride off into the sunset. It's natural for us to feel like we're playing with "house money." And wanting to experience the feel of the rush again, we keep pushing as we hope that lightning will strike twice. Investors can learn a great lesson from John Paulson, who struck lightning like nobody else before or since.

John Paulson started his hedge fund, Paulson & Co., with $2 million of his own money in 1994. He previously spent time at the investment bank Bear Stearns, where he specialized in merger arbitrage. This strategy involves simultaneously buying and selling short the stocks of two merging companies. The trade is executed based on the likelihood that the deal will close. But merger arbitrage is a relatively boring slice of the hedge fund world, and this strategy is not what put John Paulson on the map. Rather it was his massive wager, a full-on assault against the United States housing bubble. After the implosion of the housing market, his assets ballooned up to $36 billion and gave him control of the second largest hedge fund in the world. But not content with one massive trade, he kept searching for the next big score. It's been 10 years since he became the highest earning hedge fund manager ever, and since that time, he's lost nearly 75% of his assets. Today, he manages less than $10 billion, with 80% of it belonging to him and his staff.[5]

In the mid-2000s, while the rest of the country was taking out second mortgages and flipping houses, John Paulson took a less optimistic view. With the help of his star analyst Paolo Pellegrini, it became more and more likely that a bubble was inflating in the US real estate market.

If you wanted a mortgage in 2005, all you had to do was ask for one. In one instance, a mariachi singer claimed to have a six-figure income and, despite having little knowledge of what such a singer earned, the lender agreed to the loan. In lieu of official proof of income, it included a photo of him in his performance outfit.[6] Alberto and Rosa Ramirez, strawberry pickers earning $300 a week, pooled their resources with another couple, mushroom farmers who earned $500 a week. Together, with a combined salary of $3,200 a month, they got a mortgage for $3,000 a month. Strawberry pickers who earned $15,000 a year "qualified" for a $720,000 mortgage. This was the bubble in a nutshell.[7]

By 2005, $625 billion of mortgages were taken out by subprime borrowers, a fifth of all home mortgages that year, and 24% of all mortgages were originated without the borrower putting any money down.[8] Paolo Pellegrini, who was integral to the idea that there was a bubble in residential real estate, told Paulson that home prices were about to plummet. Until 2000, housing prices hadn't kept up with inflation for 25 years, averaging a 1.4% increase per year. Then, during what turned out to be the housing bubble, started inflating prices at a rate of five times their annual average. By 2005, prices had soared, and Pellegrini was convinced it was only a matter of time before they took a serious nosedive to get them back in line with their 25-year trend. With this information, Paulson was ready to go to work.[9]

The problem was that you can't short a house, so they had to figure out a different way to bet against the market. They learned about credit default swaps, insurance contracts that allow you to bet against the debt of companies. His first foray into shorting the housing market was purchasing credit default swaps on MBIA Inc., which insured mortgage bonds. For $500,000 a year, Paulson could purchase $100 million worth of insurance against the debt of MBIA Inc.[10] In 2005, he bought more credit default swaps, this time on two big lenders, Countrywide Financial and Washington Financial.

But if he thought that one of the biggest scores of all time would be easy, he quickly realized how long it could take for these things to play out. Home prices stopped rising in September 2005,[11] but his credit default swaps kept losing money.

If you're going to win the equivalent of the lottery, with returns of 1,000% or more, you have to bet against consensus. And I don't mean that one or two of your friends disagree with you. I mean *everybody* disagrees with you to the point that they think you're insane. Imagine, for example, that you think Apple is worth zero. That the entire operation is a fraud, and that the $240 billion worth of cash they say they have doesn't exist. And your belief in this is so strong that you plow your entire life savings into put options that bet against the most successful company of all time. This is what Paulson was doing in the housing market a decade ago. One hedge fund investor said, "Paulson was a merger-arb guy and suddenly he has strong views on housing and subprime. The largest mortgage guys including Vranos at Ellington, one of the gods of the market, were far more positive on subprime."[12] But Paulson didn't care about all that. He just kept buying credit default swaps like there was no tomorrow. Other traders thought Paulson was crazy and that this could be the folly that shuts him down. Interested in hearing from housing experts, Paulson brought in an analyst from Bear Stearns who assured them that they used sound models to predict mortgage solvency and housing prices. They had been carefully studying the market for two decades, and they were untroubled by Pellegrini's assessment of the housing bubble.

Paulson was confident that his team's analysis was correct, but how did he *know* he was right? How could anyone possibly know that? Everybody he spoke with outside of his team told him he was crazy. That is the emotional price that most people who say they're contrarians aren't willing to pay. People don't like to have their judgment questioned, but you can't achieve Brobdingnagian returns without people thinking you have a few screws loose.

Finally, in February 2007, Paulson received an inkling of confirmation that he was on the right side of the trade. New Century Financial, the nation's second biggest subprime lender, saw its stock free fall by 36% after announcing that it would restate its earnings for the first three quarters of 2006. As the ABX index, which measures the value of mortgages made to subprime borrowers, plummeted from 100 to 60, Paulson quickly found himself sitting on $1.25 billion of gains.

It's one thing to be right on a thesis, but to profit off of it in real time is incredibly difficult, especially if you're managing other people's money. Paulson's investors weren't happy watching him bleed, month after month and quarter after quarter. These insurance payments were going out the window with nothing to show for it in return. And then when they started to see signs that he was right and the insurance started to pay off, they pleaded with him to take profits.[13]

Investors are told to "let their winners run," but can you imagine sitting on $1 billion in profits and not selling? Could you sleep at night? What if this was just a hiccup and the index snapped back? Would giving up $1 billion of gains leave a permanent scar?

The ABX index rebounded to 77, and Paulson's gains were cut in half. But this proved to be nothing more than a dead-cat bounce, and the defaults from subprime borrowers picked up momentum. In 2007, when the subprime market imploded, Paulson's two credit funds gained 590% and 350%. Paulson & Co. earned $15 billion, and his personal rake was $4 billion. Nobody had ever made more in a single year in the history of financial markets.[14]

There are a few problems, problems that all of us hope for, when you win big in the market. After a huge score, ordinary gains no longer move the emotional needle. Paulson, like most people who experience gigantic success, quickly went searching for his next big trade. "It's like Wimbledon. When you win one year, you don't quit; you want to win again."[15] The other issue is that it's virtually impossible to have fantastic success and keep your ego in check. We're all overconfident to begin with, and huge gains make our feet levitate off the ground.

In the aftermath of the financial crisis and the Federal Reserve's quantitative easing program, Paulson turned to a new asset. He firmly believed the future would bring inflation, so he looked for something that would not be negatively impacted – in fact, he wanted to buy something that could become even more valuable in an inflationary environment. The answer was gold. So in the summer 2010, Paulson plowed $5 billion into gold-related investments, becoming the largest owner of gold in the world.

Paulson hasn't been able to repeat the success he experienced during the great financial crisis. Gold has lost 30% since its high in 2011, and Paulson & Co.'s Advantage Fund, its most high-profile offering, lost more than one-third of its value that year. The following year, the fund slipped another 14%, and it still hasn't recovered. After a 26% boost in 2013, Advantage has suffered losses three years in a row. In 2016, many of Paulson's other funds also declined. An Advantage sister fund that relies on leverage to generate steeper returns also suffered losses totaling 49% of its value. A fund specializing in mergers and arbitrage, considered Paulson's area of expertise, lost 25% of its value in 2016 alone.[16]

In 2010, Paulson was the highest-paid hedge fund manager, earning $4.9 billion.[17] That's $13.4 million a day, $559,000 an hour, $9,000 a minute, $155 a second – at least before taxes. Not that $4.9 billion needs any further context, but in 2010, the most valuable sports franchise in the world was Manchester United, coming in at $1.83 billion.[18]

At least 40 US stocks (in the Russell 3000) have doubled in each of the past five years, so there are plenty of opportunities to earn large returns. It's in our nature to look for shortcuts. Everyone wants to find the next Microsoft. But there a plethora of problems come with swinging for the fences. First of all and most obviously, they are incredibly difficult to come by. The 50 largest hedge funds do 50% of all NYSE listed stock trading, and the smallest one spends $100 million annually buying information.[19] Imagine that you were physically exchanging stock certificates with Jim Simons of Renaissance Technologies every time you went to buy or sell a stock. This is who you're playing against. The idea that you will stumble upon riches by dumb luck alone is possible, but a little naive. The second problem, and this is a problem we all wish for, is that once you've experienced outsized success in the stock market, you crave a similar rush. Earning 4% tax free in municipal bonds doesn't quite have the same feeling as earning a multithousand return.

You only need to get rich once. If you've worked hard or just got lucky and now find yourself in the top 1%, stop trying to hit home runs, you've already won.

Notes

1. Patricia Sullivan, "William 'Bud' Post III; Unhappy Lottery Winner," *Washington Post*, January 20, 2006.
2. Deborah L. Jacobs, "Winning the Lottery Isn't Always a Happy Ending," *Forbes*, November 28, 2012.
3. Ric Edelman, "Why So Many Lottery Winners Go Broke," *Fortune*, January 15, 2016.
4. Michael Mauboussin, *The Success Equation* (Boston: Harvard Business Review, 2012), 17.
5. Mike Weiss and Katharine Burton, "John Paulson Is Struggling to Hold On to Client Money," Bloomberg.com, June 5, 2017.
6. Peter S. Goodman and Gretchen Morgenson, "Saying Yes, WaMu Built an Empire on Shaky Loans," *New York Times*, December 27, 2008.
7. Carol Lloyd, "Minorities Are the Emerging Face of the Subprime Mortgage Crisis," *San Francisco Gate*, April 13, 2007.
8. Gregory Zuckerman, *The Greatest Trade Ever* (New York: Crown Business, 2010), 42–50.
9. Ibid., 107.
10. Ibid., 72.
11. S&P/Case-Shiller U.S. National Home Price Index Y/O/Y % change.
12. Ibid., 126.
13. Ibid., 209.
14. Ibid., 261.
15. Quoted in Zuckerman, *The Greatest Trade Ever*, 282.
16. Alexandra Stevenson and Matthew Goldstein, "Paulson's Fall from Hedge Fund Stardom," *New York Times*, May 1, 2017.
17. Katya Wachtel, "The Top 25 Hedge Fund Earners In 2010," *Business Insider*, April 4, 2011.
18. *Forbes*, "Most Valuable Athletes and Teams," July 21, 2010.
19. Charles D. Ellis. *The Index Revolution* (Hoboken, NJ: Wiley, 2016).

CHAPTER 14

Charlie Munger

Handling Big Losses

> You need patience, discipline, and an ability to take losses without going crazy.
>
> —Charlie Munger Kiplinger, 2005

Netflix, Amazon, and Google are three of the most successful companies over the past decade. Their products have changed the way we live, and their shareholders have in turn been rewarded with tremendous profits. That is, assuming their shareholders had the discipline to stick around. One of the oldest tenets of finance is that risk is tied with reward. If you want big rewards, you can be sure that big risk is never far behind.

Amazon is up a whopping 38,600% since its 1997 IPO, compounding at 35.5% annually. This would have grown a $1,000 investment into $387,000 today. But the degree of difficulty of *actually* turning that $1,000 into $387,000 20 years later cannot be overstated. See, Amazon got cut in half three separate times. On one of those occasions, from December 1999 through October 2001, it lost 95% of its value! Over that time, the hypothetical $1,000 investment would have shrunk from a high of $54,433 down to $3,045, a $51,388 loss. So you see why looking at a long-term winner and wishing you had bought in is a fool's errand. "Man I should have known Amazon was going to change the world." Fine, perhaps you should have. But even if you had that information, it would not have made it any easier to hang on for the ride.

Netflix, another revolutionary company, compounded at 38% since its IPO in May 2002. But this too required an almost inhuman amount of discipline to stay invested. Netflix got cut in half four times and fell 82% between July 2011 and September 2012. A $1,000 investment would have grown to $36,792, and then shrank to $6,629 over this time. Could an investor have watched their initial investment fall by thirty times over? A 500% gain over the previous 20 months went up in smoke in just 14 months!

Google, the youngest of the three companies, has compounded at more than 25% a year since it went public in 2004, delivering investors a smoother ride than in either Amazon or Netflix. Shares "only" got cut in half once, losing 65% of their value from November 2007 to November 2008. And when they did, many investors were unable to weather the storm that all of these great companies experience. Over the 265 days it took to bottom, nearly $845 billion worth of stock was bought and sold. The average market cap for Google over this time was just under $153 billion.

In other words, the stock was turned over five and a half times, robbing many investors of the 515% return over the next eight years.

Charlie Munger was never interested in investing in highfliers like Amazon, Netflix, or Google. But he, like those companies, has produced tremendous long-term results, even if he also experienced incredible short-term pain. Munger, vice chairman of Berkshire Hathaway, is famous for being the longtime partner of Warren Buffett, and he's infamous for his tremendous intellect and his aphorisms colloquially known as "Mungerisms." He is fond of inverting the problem, reverse engineering, and thinking things backward. For example, "All I want to know is where I'm going to die so I'll never go there." At the 2002 annual Berkshire Hathaway shareholder's meeting he said, "People calculate too much and think too little."

One of the traits that separates Munger from the rest of us plebeians is that he was never distracted by opportunities that were outside his circle of competence. He once said that "we have three baskets: in, out, and too tough."[1] Investors would be wise to follow his advice: "If something is hard, we move onto something else. What could be simpler than that?"[2]

In today's world where new products are coming to the market daily, it would serve investors well to recognize the purple and green lures:

> I think the reason why we got into such idiocy in investment man-agement is best illustrated by a story that I tell about the guy who sold fishing tackle. I asked him, "My god, they're purple and green. Do fish really take these lures?" And he said, "Mister, I don't sell to fish."[3]

In 1948, more than a decade prior to meeting Buffett, Munger grad-uated from Harvard Law School and went onto a successful law career, following in his father's footsteps. While he was practicing, he got into real estate development projects and earned his first million dollars. His pas-sion for investing exploded when Ed Davis, one of Buffett's first investors, introduced the two young men in 1959. Buffett asked Davis for an invest-ment of $100,000 and was surprised to get it. Davis hadn't seemed to pay very much attention to Buffett's explanation of his investment strategy, so Buffett was surprised when Davis agreed so easily. The reason was that Buffett reminded Davis of another investor, one that Davis trusted whole-heartedly: Charlie Munger. Buffett reminded Davis of Munger so much, that he even accidentally made Buffett's checks out in Munger's name![4]

Munger and Buffett hit it off right away. After years of speaking with Buffett, learning and sharing ideas of his own, in 1962, the same year that he founded a new law firm (Munger, Tolles & Olson, still around today; Charlie left in 1965), he also established what would become an incredibly successful hedge fund, Wheeler, Munger & Company.

Munger came out of the gate scalding hot. From 1962 to 1969, before fees, the fund's average annual return was a mind boggling 37.1%.[5] This is even more incredible when you think about the environment at the time. Over those eight years, picking stocks was hardly like shooting fish in a barrel. In fact, the S&P 500, including dividends, gained 6.6% over the same time. Over the fund's entire 14-year existence, Munger averaged 24% returns, compounding at 19.82% annually, well above the indexes, which gained just 5.2% over the same time, including dividends (S&P 500). Munger's limited partners would have done very well if they rode with him through thick and thin. But sticking with Munger, like sticking with Amazon, would prove no easy feat.

The best lesson investors can learn from one of the best to ever do it is that there are no good times without the bad times. Big losses are in the fabric of long-term investing. And if you're not willing to accept them, you will not harvest the long-term returns that the market has to offer. Munger once said:

> If you're not willing to react with equanimity to a market price decline of 50 percent or more two or three times a century, you're not fit to be a common shareholder and you deserve the mediocre result you're going to get compared to the people who do have the temperament, who can be more philosophical about these market fluctuations.[6]

Warren Buffett once said of Munger: "He was willing to accept greater peaks and valleys of performance, and he happens to be a fellow whose whole psyche goes toward concentration, with results shown."[7] Concentration was an understatement; Munger would make most focused investors look diversified. By the end of 1974, 61% of the fund was in Blue Chip Stamps.[8] In the bear market, the worst since the Great Depression, Blue Chip got crushed and the huge position that Munger had inflicted serious damage on his portfolio. Trading stamp revenues peaked at $124,180,000 and by 1982 sales fell to $9 million. By 2006, sales were just $25,000. "As for the original business of Blue Chip Stamps: 'I presided over a reduction in trading stamp sales from over

$120 million down to less than $100,000. So I presided over a failure of 99.99 percent.'"[9])

Blue Chip Stamps would recover and would go on to be an extremely important asset that would purchase See's Candies, the *Buffalo Evening News*, and Wesco Financial, before eventually being folded into Berkshire Hathaway in 1983.[10]

Wheeler, Munger lost 31.9% in 1973 (versus a negative 13.1% for the Dow Jones Industrial Average) and another 31.5% in 1974 (compared to a −23.1% for the Dow). Munger said: "*We got drubbed by the 1973 to 1974 crash, not in terms of true underlying value, but by quoted market value, as our publicly traded securities had to be marked down to below half of what they were really worth.* "It was a tough stretch − 1973 to 1974 was a very unpleasant stretch."[11] Munger wasn't alone, it was a tough stretch for many great investors. Shares of Buffett's Berkshire Hathaway fell from $80 in December 1972 to $40 in December 1974. The bear market of 1973–1974 sent the S&P 500 down 50% (the Dow Jones Industrial Average fell 46.6%, back to 1958 levels).

An investment of $1,000 with the great Charlie Munger on January 1, 1973, would have been worth just $467 on January 1, 1975. Munger quickly bounced back − earning 73.2% in 1975 − but not soon enough. He lost a big investor, which left him feeling mentally and emotionally depleted. He decided it was time to liquidate the partnership.

Even with the brutal performance from 1973 to 1974, the fund earned 24.3% before fees over its lifetime.

It's not just the highfliers that get cut in half. Anything that compounds for a long time must decompound at some point in time. The Dow is up 26, 400% since 1914, but it lost 30% on nine separate occasions. It lost 90% of its value during the Great Depression, and it wouldn't break through the 1929 highs until 1955. Talk about stocks for the long run! The Dow, which is the blue chip index, has suffered two massive drawdowns in the first decade of the twenty-first century (−38% in the tech bubble and −54% in the great financial crisis).

The takeaway for mere mortals like you and me is that if you seek big returns, whether they're compressed into a few years or over our investing lifetime, big losses are just part of the deal. Munger once said, "We have a passion for keeping things simple."[12] You can simplify all you want, but that still won't insulate you from large losses. Even a 50/50 stock and bond portfolio lost a quarter of its value in the Great Financial Recession.

There are several ways to think about losses. The first is absolute, how an investment stands on its own. And in Munger's case, he had quite a few absolute losses. He experienced a 53% loss while he was managing his hedge fund, and his shares in Berkshire Hathaway experienced six separate 20% drawdowns. A drawdown, for those unfamiliar, is how far an investment falls from its high. So in other words, Berkshire Hathaway has made an all-time high and subsequently lost 20% six different times.

The second type of loss is relative, that is, what you could have earned elsewhere. In the late nineties, when Internet stocks gripped the country, Berkshire kept to its circle of competence. This cost them dearly. From June 1998 through March 2000, Berkshire lost 49% of its value. If that wasn't painful enough, Internet stocks were pouring barrels of salt in the wound. Over the same time, the NASDAQ 100 rose 270%! In the 1999 Berkshire Hathaway letter, Warren Buffett wrote, "Relative results are what concern us: Over time, bad relative numbers will produce unsatisfactory absolute results."

Poor relative results are an inevitable part of investing, whether you're picking stocks or indexes. In the five years leading up to the peak of the Internet bubble, Berkshire Hathaway underperformed the S&P 500 by 117%! Charlie Munger didn't bail, but a lot of people questioned at the time whether Munger and Buffett were out of touch with the new world.

The reason why Munger's wealth has been able to compound over the past 55 years, in his own words:

> Warren and I aren't prodigies. We can't play chess blindfolded or be concert pianists. But the results are prodigious, because we have a temperamental advantage that more than compensates for a lack of IQ points.[13]

You must react to losses with equanimity. The time to sell an investment is not after it has declined in price. If this how you invest, you're destined for a long life of disappointing returns. Learn from one of the best whoever did it, and do not attempt to avoid losses. It cannot be done. Instead, focus on making sure that you're not putting yourself in a position of being a forced seller. If you know that stocks have gotten cut in half before, and undoubtedly will again in the future, make sure you don't own more than you're comfortable with. How do you do that?

Here's how. Let's say you have a portfolio that's worth $100,000 and you know that you cannot stomach losing more than $30,000. Assuming that if stocks get cut in half and that bonds will retain their value (and that definitely is an assumption, nothing is guaranteed), do not put any more than 60% of your portfolio in stocks. If that 60% gets cut in half, you should still be okay.

Notes

1. Wesco Annual Meeting, 2002.
2. Berkshire Hathaway Annual Meeting, 2006.
3. USC Business School, 1994.
4. Janet Lowe, *Damn Right! Behind the Scenes with Berkshire Hathaway Billionaire Charlie Munger* (Hoboken, NJ: Wiley, 2000), 2.
5. Ibid., 103.
6. Interview with BBC, 2012.
7. Lowe, *Damn Right!*, 100.
8. Ibid., 105.
9. Superior Court of the State of California for the County of Los Angeles, *Metropolitan News Company v. Daily Journal Corporation and Charles T. Munger*, July 1, 1999, Vol. 12, p. 1815.
10. Charles Munger, "Blue Chip Stamps Shareholder Letters 1978–1982."
11. Lowe, *Damn Right!*, 103.
12. Wesco Annual Meeting, 2002.
13. Jason Zweig, "A Fireside Chat with Charlie Munger," *Wall Street Journal*, September 12, 2014.

CHAPTER 15

Chris Sacca

Dealing with Regret

> My intention was to minimize my future regret.
>
> —Harry Markowitz

The point of this book was not to teach you how to avoid lousy investments. Rather, it is to show you that lousy investments *cannot* be avoided. Tough times are simply a part of the deal. There is not an investor alive who has hit 1,000%; in fact, nobody has come even close. One of the main reasons why consistent success eludes investors is because we simply don't have much experience making financial decisions. *Homo sapiens* have been around for thousands of generations, hunting and gathering and protecting the nest. Investing and saving for retirement, however, is something very foreign to us, and we're only now just learning some of the rules.

The New York Stock Exchange opened in 1817, less than 10 generations ago. Index funds are only 40 years old. If you were to plot the two-million-year-old history of *Homo sapiens* on a single day, modern portfolio theory would appear at 11:59:58. Framing it this way, Michael Mauboussin asked, "What have you learned in the past two seconds?"[1]

Human beings' primary motivation over the past two million years has been to pass our genes onto the next generation. Simple rules of thumb like "if you hear something in the bushes, run" has aided our efforts in doing this. If it turned out that the noise wasn't a saber-tooth tiger but only wind, no harm no foul. This "run first, ask questions later" attitude is something that helped us survive in the field, but too many people have been unable to suppress this primal instinct from their investment decisions. This has and will continue to create a wedge between investment returns and investor returns. Running at the first sign of trouble in financial markets is dangerous because it's almost never a saber-toothed tiger and the "no harm no foul" rules don't apply in financial markets.

The average intra-year decline for US stocks is 14%, so a little wind in the bushes is to be expected.[2] But saber-toothed tigers, or backbreaking bear markets, are few and far between. Corrections occur all the time, but rarely do they turn into something worse, so selling every time stocks fall a little and waiting for the dust to settle is a great way to buy high and sell low. In the past 100 years, we've experienced just a handful of truly awful markets; the Great Depression, the post-go-go years meltdown, the 1973–1974 bear, the dot-com bubble bursting, and most recently, the great financial crisis. Selling every time stocks fall a little is no way to invest because you'd live in a constant state of regret, and regret is one of the most destructive emotions in the cognitive-bias tool kit.

Investors don't just exist in the present state, they carry past experiences with them. This is dangerous because it leads us to constantly draw parallels where none exist. Looking at each decision independent of previous ones would be beneficial because investors are overly reliant on past experiences when thinking about future scenarios. To test this hypothesis, a team of researchers studied brain-damaged individuals with normal IQs. The parts of the brain responsible for logic were intact, but the areas responsible for emotions was damaged, which limited their ability to experience ordinary feelings such as stress, regret, and anxiety. The *Wall Street Journal* reported on this link in 2005:

> The study suggests the participants' lack of emotional responsiveness actually gave them an advantage when they played a simple investment game. The emotionally impaired players were more willing to take gambles that had high payoffs because they lacked fear. Players with undamaged brain wiring, however, were more cautious and reactive during the game, and wound up with less money at the end.[3]

Even if we were told that a loaded coin would land on heads 60% of the time, seeing four tails in a row would alter some people's decisions, despite knowing that they should bet on heads every single time. "If you just observe these people, they know the right thing to do.... But when they actually get into the game, they start reacting to the outcomes of the previous rounds."

Humans come preprogrammed with something called hindsight bias. It's a defect in our software that falsely leads us to believe we knew what was going to happen all along, when in reality we had no clue. Hindsight bias leads to regret, and regret leads to poor decision making. Regret steers our brain in two distinct ways: We do nothing out of fear that we'll make the wrong decision. "I'm going to hold onto this fund that's done horribly because I can't stand the thought of selling at the bottom," and it can compel us to do something because we don't want to regret *not* doing it: "I'm going to buy this ICO (initial coin offering) because I won't be able to live with myself if I miss the next Bitcoin."

You know Steve Jobs and his early partner Steve Wozniak, but the name Ronald Wayne likely means nothing to you. Wayne was the third founder of Apple, but the reason his name is erased from the history books is because in 1976 he sold his 10% stake in the company for $800.[4]

Apple is currently worth north of $900 billion! You're never going to experience anything quite this painful, but the odds are high that at some point in time, you'll pass on an investment that goes on to deliver fantastic results. You cannot avoid regrets in this game. You'll buy stuff you wish you hadn't and sell things you wish you held onto. We can learn all about regret by studying one of the most successful investors of all time, Chris Sacca, who has arguably left more money on the table than anyone in the twenty-first century. There are only eight private companies currently valued at 10 billion or more. Chris Sacca passed on two of them.[5]

A 10-bagger is an investment that multiplies an initial investment 10 times. Most investors won't be lucky enough to find this needle in a haystack, but even if they do, most will lack the discipline to ever turn $1 into $10. It's extremely difficult to watch something that has gone up so much without feeling (a) greedy and (b) that the gains will be ripped away from you. While 10 baggers are the unicorn in public markets, in private markets, especially at the early stage, thousand baggers exist. Chris Sacca and his investors have experienced this perhaps more times than anybody in the history of private or public investing.

Sacca is the founder and chairman of Lowercase Capital, an early stage venture capital fund. In a conversation with Tim Ferriss, Sacca said his first fund "might be the most successful fund in the history of venture capital."[6] With returns of 250 times their original investment, his early investors hit the mother lode. Having your money grow 250 times is an incredible accomplishment. For comparison, in order to have earned a 250 times return on your investment in Apple, one of the best-performing stocks of all time, you would have had to buy the stock all the way back in February 1998!

Sacca became a billionaire in under 10 years and before the age of 40 because he is an expert at spotting unicorns, private companies that have reached the $1 billion valuation mark.

Lowercase Capital was one of the first investors in Uber, putting $300,000 into the concept. Recently, it owned as much as 4% of the company, giving the fund a 5,000 bagger.[7]

Some of Sacca's other home runs include Instagram, Uber, Kickstarter, Slack, Automattic (WordPress parent company), Twilio, and most notably, Twitter. By the time of the initial public offering, he and Sacca's funds had accumulated 18% of the company. He originally invested in Twitter at a $5 million valuation,[8] and it's currently valued at $15 billion, giving Sacca a 3,000 bagger. His Twitter investment has reportedly returned an astonishing $5 billion for his investors.[9] Sacca invested in Instagram's Series A at a $20,000,000 valuation,[10] which was later purchased by Facebook for $1 billion, giving Sacca "only" a 50 bagger.

Sacca has four rules of investing, which he shared on *The Tim Ferriss Show* podcast:

1. He must know that he can have a direct and personal impact on the outcome.
2. The investment must be excellent before he gets involved. Sacca looks to make good things better. He doesn't try to fix something that's not good to begin with.
3. He allows time for a deal to make him rich.
4. He selects deals he will be proud of and commits to them.[11]

Even an investor with a process and fantastic returns doesn't go to sleep without a few regrets. Sacca has had the opportunity to invest in some of the most successful start-ups of the twenty-first century. Many he jumped on and regrettably, others he passed on.

Sacca met Nick Woodman, the founder of GoPro, while he was working at Google. He didn't have his fund at the time, but he would have passed on investing if given the opportunity. He told Tim Ferriss the story: "Eric Schmidt, CEO of Google said, 'Hey, will you come in here and sit with this pitch? A friend of a friend said we gotta meet this guy.' Woodman comes in with GoPro and Eric's like 'I don't know,' and I was like we'd be foolish to do this deal. How's this guy from Santa Cruz gonna compete with all these Asians building hardware? You can't hold a candle to the Taiwanese and the Koreans. I was like no dice man, let this guy go." GoPro went public in 2014 at a valuation just below $3 billion.[12]

He didn't have the chance to invest in GoPro, but Sacca said no to some of the most well-known and storied businesses of the decade. "One of my constant recurring nightmares is about the stuff I passed on." He tells a story about the time he met with Dropbox, whom he met while they were still in Y Combinator's early-stage start-up program. He didn't think they could beat Google, which was developing its own file-sharing service, Drive. He went so far as to recommend that Dropbox pursue a different path. Lucky for Dropbox, they didn't take his advice. Sacca estimates his decision to not invest in Dropbox cost him "hundreds of millions of dollars."[13] At close to a $10 billion valuation, Dropbox is one of the biggest misses of Sacca's career.

Chris Sacca spoke to Bill Simmons about another miss – passing on Snap, the parent company of Snapchat. At the time, Snapchat was widely considered to be an app ideal for sending photos that are not safe for work. Images sent on Snapchat (called *Snaps*) automatically disappear seconds after they are viewed. Snap continued developing new functionality, so today users can create Stories, a series of photos that don't disappear. Sacca couldn't see Snap's potential and passed.[14] Now, Snapchat functions like a full social media or messaging app, and it has a huge user base, especially among Generation Z. Snap went public in 2017 at a $24 billion valuation.[15] Ouch.

When Simmons asked, "Is that your biggest misfire?" Sacca responded, "I misfire all the time. I told the Airbnb guys what they're doing is unsafe and somebody was gonna get raped and murdered in a shared house."[16] Airbnb is currently worth more than $30 billion.[17]

Sacca is able to speak openly and candidly about his misses because he's had so many winners. He understands that swinging and missing, or in these cases watching the pitch and not swinging is part of the game. For us mere mortals however, passing on the next Amazon, or selling it too early can have disastrous and long-lasting effects, because for us, these opportunities don't come around too often. Sacca is able to look at these missed opportunities and move on, whereas most people would be left with a giant scar.

Regret is highly correlated with emotional extremes, and emotional extremes happen when you have either big embedded gains or losses. You put $10,000 into a stock, and it doubled, now what? You're afraid that if you sell you'll leave money on the table and also that if you hold it, your gains will evaporate. You put $10,000 into a stock and it got cut in half. Now what? If you sell, you know that will mark the low, but if you hold, who knows how low it can go? Whenever I speak to somebody in this position, I always ask this question: What would feel worse – you hold onto the stock and it gets cut in half, or you sell it and it doubles again? Neither of these would feel too great, but holding onto a stock and watching all the gains disappear is more mentally straining than locking in gains only to watch the stock go higher. It's easy to tell yourself that you were just being prudent, that it would have been irresponsible not to sell. It's hard to tell yourself that you held onto a stock that doubled because you thought it would double again.

We can't know what the future holds, so it's crucial that we minimize regret. Harry Markowitz who practically invented modern portfolio theory once spoke about how regret drove his own asset allocation: "I visualized my grief if the stock market went way up and I wasn't in it – or it went way down and I was completely in it. My intention was to minimize my future regret."[18]

The best way to minimize future regret when you have big gains or losses is to sell some. There's no right amount, but for example, if you sell 20% and the stock doubles, hey, at least you still have 80% of it. On the other hand, if the stock gets cut in half, hey, at least you sold some of it. People tend to think in all or nothing terms, but it doesn't have to be that way. Thinking in absolutes is almost guaranteed to end with regret. Minimize regret and you'll maximize the chances of you being a successful investor over the long term.

Notes

1. VW Staff, "Michael Mauboussin: What Have You Learned in the Past 2 Seconds?," *ValueWalk*, February 6, 2015.
2. J. P. Morgan, "Guide to the Markets," November 30, 2017.
3. Jane Spencer, "Lessons from the Brain-Damaged Investor," *Wall Street Journal*, July 21, 2005.
4. Jessica Chia, "Apple Co-founder Who Sold His 10 Percent Stake for Just $800 Has Never Owned Any of the Company's Products and Insists He Doesn't Regret a Thing," *Daily Mail*, July 13, 2017.
5. Scott Austin, Chris Canipe, and Sarah Slobin, "The Billion Dollar Startup Club," *Wall Street Journal*, February 18, 2015.
6. Chris Sacca, interview with Tim Ferriss, *The Tim Ferriss Show* podcast, October 29, 2015.
7. Jillian D'Onfro, "Investor That Owns 4% of Uber 'Barely Speaks' with Uber's CEO," *Business Insider*, March 25, 2015.
8. Crunchbase, "Series A – Twitter," December 2017.
9. Yolanda's Little Black Book, "Billionaire Chris Sacca's Baller Real Estate Portfolio," December 15, 2016.
10. Crunchbase, "Series A – Instagram," December 2017.
11. Interview with Tim Ferriss.
12. Neha Dimri, "GoPro's IPO Priced at $24 per Share: Underwriter," Reuters, June 25, 2014.
13. Interview with Tim Ferriss.

14. Chris Sacca, interview with Bill Simmons, "Episode 95: Billionaire Investor Chris Sacca," *The Bill Simmons Podcast*, April 28, 2016.
15. Portia Crowe, "Snap Is Going Public at a $24 Billion Valuation," *Business Insider*, March 1, 2017.
16. Interview with Bill Simmons.
17. Lauren Thomas, "Airbnb Just Closed a $1 Billion Round and Became Profitable in 2016," CNBC.com, March 9, 2017.
18. SEI, "Behavioral Finance: Loss and Regret Aversion," September 2014.

CHAPTER 16

Michael Batnick

Looking in the Mirror

You will do a great disservice to yourselves, to your clients, and to your businesses, if you view behavioral finance mainly as a window onto the world. In truth, it is also a mirror that you must hold up to yourselves.

—Jason Zweig

Earlier in the book I highlighted one of Stanley Druckenmiller's unforced errors; I've committed literally thousands of them. You might think this is hyperbole. It isn't. In 2012, I spent $12,000 in trading commissions. It's hard to believe I was trading that frequently; at the time, I thought I was investing! The following year, I decided to slow things down and focus on the big picture, with a slower, longer-term approach. I lost almost $12,000 in a year when US stocks rose 32%. I've made almost every mistake in this book.

I have traded individual stocks from Alcoa to Zynga, basket of stocks both domestic and international (ETFs), bonds, currencies (ETFs), and commodities (ETFs). The "thought process" wasn't always the same. I've tried putting all the macro pieces together like John Maynard Keynes and I've tried valuing companies on the micro level like Benjamin Graham. I've been overconfident. I've anchored to my purchase price. I've cut my winners short and let my losers run. I made a lifetime of mistakes and was fortunate enough to do them in a small window of time. It takes some people decades to figure out what works for them, and many just never get there. How was I able to jam pack my failures into just a few years? Let's go back to the beginning.

I wasn't one of those kids who bought their first stock when they were 11 years old. I didn't read the *Wall Street Journal* in high school, and I didn't build algorithms in my dorm room. In fact, the way I treated education is the biggest regret I have in life.

I didn't take high school seriously, but I got by and did well enough on my SATs to get into a good business school. When I went to college, I was in over my head. I spent a lifetime going through the motions, so looking back, it's not surprising that I wasn't ready, because I did nothing to *get* ready. I only lived in Indiana, but I didn't actually attend school there. It's amazing what happens to your grades when you don't go to class. I got a 1.2 GPA my first semester and followed that up with a 1.1, which apparently was unacceptable. The higher-ups told me to take some time off and reapply in a year.

I came home and went to community college for a year. With a little effort, I got my grades up and was accepted back for my junior year. But I still wasn't ready, emotionally or mentally or otherwise, and when I dropped calculus, I was summarily dismissed. This one hurt. In hindsight, there's something not so terrible about hitting rock bottom at 20 years old, but at the time, it was completely humiliating. I came home again and this time it was permanent. I remember sitting in the car with my father, tears running down my face and without any answers for him. He wasn't angry, more like disappointed, which is far worse. I didn't know what I was thinking, and I still struggle to come up with answers.

The reality of my failures hit me hard. For the first time in my life, I was thinking about my future and wondering what it would look like. A year and a half late, I finished college with a degree in economics, but I still had no idea what I wanted to do for a living. My nascent professional career wasn't helped by the fact that it was 2008 and millions of Americans were losing their jobs.

Shortly after I graduated, I got a job at a financial planning company. I felt like the luckiest kid in the world. I had screwed up royally in college and was no worse for the wear. But what I thought I signed up for and what I actually signed up for were two entirely different things. The job was all about selling insurance to anybody you knew and cold calling everybody you didn't know. I did that for about a year and a half, and it was a lousy experience. I was given no salary, was required to pay rent (not a typo), and had no desire to pretend to prepare a financial plan for someone and then use insurance products to deliver the plan. I purchased a policy for my wife and myself, my dad bought something, and that was that. I didn't sell anything else in those 18 months. I was paying for my big mistake, and those tuition payments would continue for a few more years.

While I was at the insurance company, my father introduced me to a real financial adviser. The guy took a liking to me and started sharing sell-side research reports with me every day. I had no idea what "PIIGS" (Portugal, Ireland, Italy, Greece, Spain) were, but I enjoyed the material and decided this was what I wanted to do. I didn't know exactly what "this" was, but I knew I wanted to be on Wall Street. So I quit my job and decided to get a real education. I spent every day at the library, studying for the CFA (Chartered Financial Analyst) exam, reading finance books, and catching up for lost time. I became obsessed. I was on a mission. I would find my way into the industry come hell or high water. But there were a few challenges I'd have to overcome; my résumé was garbage, the financial world was in free fall, and my mother was dying.

Every day in 2010, I would drive my girlfriend (now wife) to the train station in the morning, and I'd spend all day working. My job was to teach myself about the industry and to one day have something to offer. I passed level 1 of the CFA exam and was feeling pretty good. I was sending my résumé all over the place, but I should have done more. I wish I had the chutzpah to email strangers and walk into branches, but I didn't yet have the confidence to do that.

In 2011, I sat for level 2 of the CFA exam. When I took the test, I said to myself, "How many people in this room have zero industry experience?" For the first time in my life, I was proud of myself. I went from somebody who thought education was a joke to a laser-focused learning machine. But the test went horribly, and I knew when I walked out that I didn't pass. My mother died a few days later. It was the hardest thing I've ever experienced.

When my mother passed, she left me and my siblings some money. I had already read Jack Bogle's *The Little Book of Common Sense Investing,* and the idea of an index fund made a lot of sense to me. But I also read Jack Schwager's *Market Wizards* and the idea of becoming the next Paul Tudor Jones was much more appealing.

This was 2011, and the markets were incredibly volatile. So I did what any reasonable person with no experience does when markets are acting like a roller coaster, I started trading 3x levered ETFs. If you're not familiar with what these are, they're baskets of stocks that moves three times as much as the underlying does. So, for example, if the S&P 500 falls 1% in day, there are bull and bear ETFs that will fall or gain 3% alongside it. It's a legal gambling on steroids. My process was as follows: I would pick one of these products, my weapon of choice was FAZ (bearish banks), buy it, watch the price, and hope it went up. I thought that by trading a lot, I could control my destiny. I would later find out that this cognitive bias is so common that there's a name for it; it's called "the illusion of control." By buying and selling within minutes or hours of each other, I wouldn't be held hostage to the market. It's hard to put into words the level of dumb this line of thinking is. Overtrading is probably the most common mistake that novice investors make, and I was no exception.

A few months later I caught a break—employment. It was only a temporary position, but I was happy just to have a paycheck. I wouldn't have the luxury of being in front of my computer during market hours, so I moved onto options. At the time, I was bearish on Netflix. I thought their streaming options stunk, and I didn't understand why they were splitting their streaming and physical DVDs into two separate plans. I bought put options a few days before they were set to release earnings. The stock fell 35% in a single day, and I made more than 10 times my original investment. I was hooked on weekly options. The problem was I was always buying options, not selling them, and 76% of all options held to expiration expire worthless.[1] It didn't take me too long to figure out what was going on here. I threw in the towel on options relatively quickly.

After my temp position expired, I went back to the library, reading and studying, but mostly trading. I was all over the place. I read books on technical analysis, I studied traditional valuation metrics, and I watched financial television for coverage of economic indicators like nonfarm payrolls. My process was chaos. I was slowly coming around to the idea that Bogle was onto something, that beating the market is a fool's errand. I'm not sure I would have come to this realization as quickly as I had if it were not for Twitter. I was pretty deep in the trading community, watching people's tweets, following their calls, and seeing what they would say when the market went against them and when it went in their favor.

It became apparent real fast that 99.9% of these people were charlatans. It was as sad as it was pathetic, and I didn't want to become one of these people who spent every day on the Internet, pretending that they were crushing the market when it was so obvious to a novice like myself that the exact opposite was happening. I watched people who dedicated their lives to the market looking like fools on a daily basis. I paid attention to everything that was going on that could move markets, and I realized that, even if you had tomorrow's news today, you wouldn't be able to consistently figure out how markets would react. There wasn't an "ah-ha" moment, it was more like a building realization that this game is really, really hard. Legendary financier Bernard Baruch captured this idea perfectly:

> If you are ready to give up everything else and study the whole history and background of the market and all principal companies whose stocks are on the board as carefully as a medical student studies anatomy- if you can do all that and in addition you have the cool nerves of a gambler, the sixth sense of a clairvoyant and the courage of a lion, you have a ghost of a chance.[2]

I was growing less and less enchanted with the market and couldn't stop thinking about how I was paying for my earlier mistakes. And then one day I got an email. A friend got me an interview as an internal wholesaler at a big asset management company. Here was my shot.

I always had this irrational confidence, and I say irrational because I never did anything to deserve to be confident, but I felt that if someone would just give me a chance, that I could make a good impression. I finally was given this opportunity. I met with somebody on the team, and it went great. I was enthusiastic, and he was talking to me about the next steps as if they were a formality, like the job was already mine. Then he took me to talk with his boss and again, we had a great conversation. And then I was asked why I wanted to be an internal wholesaler.

For those of you who don't know, an internal wholesaler is the behind-the-scenes person for the external wholesaler. The external wholesaler is the person who meets people who allocate assets. It's the external's job to meet advisers and explain to them why their products deserve a place in their client's portfolios. The internal is busy setting the external's calendar and generally acting as a right-hand person. So, when the hiring manager asked me why I wanted to be an internal wholesaler, my response was pretty far off the mark. I told him that I loved the markets, and that studying for the CFA prepared me for this role. "Whoa, whoa, whoa, stop the clock," he said. "Why are you studying for the CFA?" This pretty much ended my chances. The CFA was for analysts, not internal wholesalers, I was auditioning for the wrong role. I was crushed. Here I thought that I needed the CFA designation to give myself a chance to get into the industry, and it ended up keeping me out.

I went back to the library, trading, investing, reading, and hoping. At this point, I was pretty much fooling myself. I knew that I couldn't beat the market, but I kept trying because I didn't know what else to do. My natural network didn't have many connections to finance, and even if they did, the job market was bone dry and I didn't have much to offer. A few months went by, and I was given another opportunity. This time, it was at a discount brokerage. The role sounded perfect, and I was so excited.

The meeting went great, and the next day I got a call from the person who interviewed me. He told me what I had been hoping to hear for months: "You don't have much experience, but I like you, and I'm going to take a chance on you." I was on cloud nine. And then I was crushed. My résumé was sent through HR, and they called to ask about a ding on my credit report. I didn't know what they were talking about but promised to get to the bottom of it. During what should have been my junior year in Indiana, I had already committed to a living situation. I was working as a waiter while going to college at home, paying rent every month, and not thinking anything of it. Turns out, one of my roommates didn't pay for some damages, and this made its way onto my credit report. In the few days that it took for me to figure this out, the guy who hired me left to take a job at a different company. I was told the new manager would give me a shot. He never did. This one really hurt.

Back to the library. I started wondering if I was refusing to face the facts. That a career in finance just wasn't in the cards. "Why do you think all these kids kill themselves in high school and college? Who do you think you are that you can skip to the head of the line? Grow up, move on." I came close. Not that I ever had a plan for what a different career would be, but mentally I was close to throwing in the towel. I was still paying for a lifetime of eschewing education.

I received a third legitimate opportunity, this time outside of finance. I didn't really care because I had gone two years without a job, and I just wanted to get on with my life. It was now two years without a job, and I just wanted to get on with my life. The person interviewing me asked me what I was doing and why I was out of work for so long. I explained my situation, was told to be careful trading options, and was quickly dismissed. The "interview" lasted about three minutes.

A few days later I was in Madison Square Garden for game three of the Knicks/Heat series. As I sat down, I saw an email. Not that I didn't know this was coming, but it was a "thanks but no thanks and good luck." The Knicks were down 2–0 in the series and were getting killed, so I decided to get the hell out of there. I just wanted to go home.

It was late in the evening, and I was riding the Long Island Railroad, head buried in my BlackBerry, and scrolling through Twitter. My favorite follow, Josh Brown, is tweeting. "So, Zoë Kravitz is an adult, and Francis Bean Cobain is a teen ... and then 6 years pass, we get a bit older." This tweet is five years old; it only has one retweet, one reply, and zero likes, but this one is burned into my memory. As the train pulls into my station, my phone died. This detail is important because if it wasn't dead, I probably would have been walking with my head buried in it and not paying attention as the person who would change the entire trajectory of my life walked right past me. I walked passed Josh and froze; this was what I had been waiting for. Here was my opportunity on a silver platter.

I tapped Josh on the shoulder, and he was kind enough to give me a few minutes. I explained to him my situation; he gave me his card and said to stay in touch. My wife was waiting downstairs to pick me up, and she said to me, "Who was that?" "That's Josh Brown," I said. "The guy from Twitter I was telling you about." To put it in terms she would understand (my wife is a reality-TV fan), I said, "He's my Bethenny Frankel."

A few weeks later, Josh put up a blog post that he and Barry were hiring. I emailed him, we hit it off, and I was hired by the person who if given the opportunity to work with anybody in the world, I would have selected. When I started with Josh and Barry in 2012, they were managing around $50 million, and it was just the two of them and an assistant. Five years later, I own part of a real business. We have $700 million that we're responsible for, and employ 20 people.

A lot of people will credit their success to luck, but you can usually tell when they're full of it, when it's a thin veil of false humility shrouded on top of a giant ego. I think it's pretty apparent how lucky I am to be where I am. Sure I made my own luck. I went up to Josh, I spent months and years studying the market and building up enough knowledge to show him that I was worth taking a chance on. But if I never told the hiring manager that I was studying for the CFA, if my credit report didn't have a ding on it, if the Knicks weren't getting blown out, if Josh wasn't on the same train as I was at 11 p.m. on a weeknight, I absolutely would not be writing this book. There is no doubt in my mind that I am extremely lucky to be where I am today.

I learned a lot of ways to fail not just at life, but in the market as well. It's hard to single out the "biggest mistake" I ever made because if there's one thing I did right when I was trading, it's that I cut my losses short. I didn't take any hits that were greater than 1% of my trading account. What stands out to me, as far as lessons I've learned in the market, is that if you have a liability coming due in the next few months or even few years, do not invest.

I knew that I had two big financial commitments coming up: In December 2013, I had a wedding to pay for, and a year or two after that, I would be buying a house. I didn't want to sit in cash, so instead of putting aside money that I was going to need, I remained fully invested, and hedged by shorting the S&P 500, leaving me about 80% net long. This is not smart. The market doesn't care about your goals. It doesn't know that you're retiring in five years, when your child is going to college, or in my case, when you're getting married.

One of my investing heroes Peter Bernstein once said, "Mistakes are an inevitable part of the process." (https://www.youtube.com/watch?v=MKcZtvwch1w) He couldn't be more right. I've made plenty of mistakes in investing and in life, and I'm fine with that. A perfect history in either endeavor has never been achieved. The next time you take a big loss or sell too early or try to get back to even, remember, we've *all* been there. The difference between normal people and the best investors is that the great ones learn and grow from their mistakes, while normal people are set back by them.

Notes

1. Joe Summa, "Do Option Sellers Have a Trading Edge?" Investopedia.
2. Quoted in Ray Dalio, *Principles* (New York: Simon & Schuster, 2017), 34–35.

About the Author

Michael Batnick, CFA®, is the Director of Research at Ritholtz Wealth Management, a Registered Investment Advisor firm based out of New York City, with offices located across the country. As a member of the investment committee, he is responsible for the construction of client portfolios. Michael became a CFA charterholder in 2015.

In his spare time he enjoys reading and spending time with his wife Robyn, son Koby, and dog Bianca.

Index